SIMON SHERIDAN

Shakespeare

The Journey into the Sacred

First edition

This book was professionally typeset on Reedsy.
Find out more at reedsy.com

Contents

Prologue 1
Introduction 3
Identity and Transformation 11
Much Ado About Nothing 28
Romeo and Juliet 47
Hamlet 65
Macbeth 85
Othello 103
King Lear 120
The Tempest 144
Conclusion: King Lear vs Oedipus 160
About the Author 173
Also by Simon Sheridan 174

Prologue

There are numerous books in existence that claim to teach how to read Shakespeare or which explore the meanings of the works directly. I had no intention of adding to the list, not least because I don't have the advantage of being an established name with an official position that designates me as an authority worthy of being listened to. Indeed, I never set out to write this book. I thought I was writing a different one, one that utilised Shakespeare's works but which was not primarily about them. While writing that book, I fell backwards into this one and, like Alice, discovered the most wonderful of rabbit holes.

What I learned down the rabbit hole was that my understanding of Shakespeare had been wrong. Since that understanding did not stray far from the default interpretations that are present in our culture, it followed that my re-evaluation brought me into conflict with many of the biggest names who have written on the Bard, including such giants as Coleridge, Goethe, A.C. Bradley, and Harold Bloom.

All of these great thinkers came to a halt before the two works that they nevertheless regard as Shakespeare's greatest: Hamlet and King Lear. The perceived inexplicability of these plays led Coleridge to conclude that Shakespeare was merely using artistic licence as a vehicle for expression. It led Samuel Johnson, Voltaire, and T.S. Eliot to conclude that the works themselves were faulty. It led Bloom to conclude that the stories were "mythological" in nature, forever relegated to a mystical realm on a par with religious texts. My big discovery was that all of these interpretations are wrong. I realised how to understand King Lear and Hamlet on their own terms. The answers are right there in the stories themselves; we just need to know how to interpret them.

The key to interpretation can be summarised in the phrase which forms the title of this book, "The Journey into the Sacred". This may sound like the exact quasi-mystical terminology I have just argued against, but it is actually a technical term about the way stories work, especially Shakespeare's stories. That is what this book aims to demonstrate: a rigorous and repeatable approach to understanding Shakespeare.

But this approach should in no way extinguish the wonder we feel at Shakespeare's works, which stand by themselves as complete and perfect wholes. Nothing written here can improve them or change them in any way. The goal of this book is to change the way we view Shakespeare.

It's perfectly fitting that we would need to change ourselves in order to understand the Bard. It is a key feature of his greatest heroes. It's that transformation process that we call the *journey into the sacred* and it is the key to unlocking the meaning of Shakespeare's individual works and his *oeuvre* as a whole. That is what will be demonstrated in this book.

Introduction

More than four hundred years after his death, it would be easy to imagine that there isn't anything more to be said about the works of the man who is arguably the greatest writer in the English language. Everybody knows Shakespeare. Every schoolkid is made to read him. There are festivals, book clubs, academic conferences, countless movie adaptations, continuous performances by theatre troupes constructed exclusively for the purpose, and a voluminous secondary literature. And yet, as hard as it may be to believe, the vast majority of what has been written about Shakespeare's work misses the point and is often just plain wrong.

Perhaps harder to believe is that the root cause of the problem goes back almost exactly two thousand years before Shakespeare's time. The founder of Western philosophy, Plato, famously railed against artists for their use of fantasy and illusion, which he believed distracted from the proper pursuit of truth. Plato's student, Aristotle, took a more objective approach to the subject and set out to try and determine how art worked. His work *Poetics* would remain the foremost treatise on the subject for more than two millennia. Nevertheless, the intellectual tradition handed down from antiquity sided with Plato in that it saw art as being, at best, an inferior form not capable of expressing the highest truths about the world and, at worst, a purveyor of downright falsehood. That's why Aristotle's *Poetics* was not improved upon. Thinkers and philosophers thought the subject unworthy of attention.

The situation began to change with the rise of the Romantic movement in the late 18th century, and it is no coincidence that Shakespeare was the most important influence on a new set of thinkers who no longer saw art as an inferior form but as something capable of communicating core truths about human existence. Although we have no record of his direct thoughts on the matter, it is clear that Shakespeare believed that too, since his works contain a number of jabs at the philosophers and their tired old ways. The famous line from Hamlet sums up his attitude: "There are more things in heaven and earth, Horatio, than are dreamt of in your philosophy." What Shakespeare expressed in his plays were those things which had been left out of philosophy.

The Romantic movement set out to try and identify what even Plato had grudgingly recognised, which is that there is something to art, some deeper truth that has only been whispered in vague, quasi-mystical language, away from the mainstream Western intellectual tradition. Art presents us with a seeming paradox. It is clearly an illusion, and yet the illusion seems sometimes more real than reality. That is why Plato objected to it so strongly. Shakespeare knew perfectly well the dangers involved in these illusions, but he also knew that excessive philosophising had its own set of problems. More importantly, it seems certain that Shakespeare knew that what he was communicating with his works was not just something that philosophy had ignored but which can quite likely not be expressed at all in intellectual terms. He arguably had the same attitude to philosophy that Plato once had towards art.

Therein lies the most important reason to understand Shakespeare. It is not a matter of correcting errors in our understanding of the works themselves. That is merely the first step. What we are searching for is a new way to approach Shakespeare that unlocks the deeper truths of the human condition contained in his works. We will not try to translate Shakespeare into philosophy; we will show why it is all but impossible to do so.

To get at these more fundamental meanings, we must first correct the primary errors of understanding in the works themselves. The main form of misinterpretation that intellectual critics and commentators have made down through the centuries is to read into Shakespeare their own ideological biases. This problem has become even more prevalent in our time, with post-modernism making it a virtue to simply construct your own interpretation.

To demonstrate, let's take the two works of Shakespeare that have been the most problematic: Hamlet and King Lear. The behaviour of the heroes of these stories has caused consternation ever since the plays were first performed. In fact, King Lear was perceived as such an unrelentingly depressing work that a completely different version of the story was published by Nahum Tate in 1681 and became the dominant stage production for one hundred and fifty years afterwards, even though the meaning of the story had been completely altered by changing it from a tragedy to a comedy.

Those who weren't simply horrified by the original version of Lear expressed disbelief and incomprehension at the behaviour of the king. No less an authority than Samuel Taylor Coleridge had this to say about it:-

> *"...many obvious improbabilities will be endured, as belonging to the groundwork of the story rather than to the drama itself, in the first scenes, which would disturb or disentrance us from all illusion in the acme of our excitement; as for instance, Lear's division of his kingdom, and the banishment of Cordelia."*

Coleridge sees Lear's behaviour in the opening scene as "improbable" but allows this by ascribing it the status of "groundwork" of the story and not something to be taken seriously. Note that he invokes the idea that art is an illusion and implies that this gives the playwright leeway in the representation of events. For Coleridge, Lear's inexplicable behaviour at the start of the story is just the necessary technical means to get the plot going, nothing more.

Let's take the liberty of translating Coleridge's thought process into a simple statement. What he is saying is something like this:

I don't understand Lear's behaviour; therefore, it must be artistic licence on the part of Shakespeare.

The observation that Lear's behaviour doesn't make sense is uncontroversial. Almost everybody has that reaction. It is this ambiguity and uncertainty that creates the need to find an explanation in the first place. Why is Lear behaving this way? The question demands an answer. Coleridge's reasoning is to speculate about Shakespeare's artistic intentions. He answers the question,

"Why is Lear behaving in this way?" by creating another question, "Why is Shakespeare presenting us with a character who doesn't make sense?" He does not attempt to answer the question within the story. He jumps out of the story and deals instead with the artistic intentions of its creator.

The ambiguous behaviour of other people is a common occurrence in everyday life, and if we are in a position to ask them directly why they are acting in such a way, they can simply tell us, and the matter is resolved. It is where we are unable to start a dialogue that we fall back to speculation. This happens all the time with politicians and other celebrities who we have no direct relationship with. Clearly, it is not possible to ask the character in a fictional story to clarify his behaviour. But it is also not possible to ask Shakespeare what he meant by the character's behaviour since Shakespeare is no longer with us. All we end up with are speculations that cannot be conclusively resolved.

In terms of interpreting a work of art, the main problem with such speculations is that as soon as we go off theorising about the artist's intentions, we are no longer paying attention to the story itself. If we turn this into a habit, we may eventually find that our focus becomes entirely on the author. This actually happened in the 20th century. Following the advent of psychoanalysis, entire books were written purporting to reverse engineer the psychology of authors based on their works. Whether this approach has any validity at all (I don't believe it does), it does not deal with the work of art in the way that the author intended it to be experienced. Therefore, it undermines the very basis of art. If our goal is to understand Shakespeare, we must be wary of falling into this speculative trap.

Let's call this way of dealing with ambiguity in a work of art *reasoning back to the author*, i.e., speculating on the author's intentions. There is another pattern which is even more common, and that is *reasoning back to the character of the hero*. This practice became especially prominent with the rise of the Romantic movement. We find it in Coleridge, Schlegel, Goethe, A.C. Bradley and many others. Applied to King Lear, the reasoning goes as follows:

"I don't understand Lear's behaviour; therefore, he must be going mad/se-

nile."

This reading is far more permissible because the facts of the story support it. Lear's behaviour is overtly emotional and seemingly irrational, and he is shown as an old and physically fragile man. The conclusion that he is losing his mind makes sense. The only problem is, it's wrong. As we will show later in the book, this false conclusion sits at the heart of the misunderstanding of Lear that persists to this day. This is one example of where *reasoning back to the character of the hero* can lead us astray.

A second example is Hamlet. Hamlet's behaviour has been seen to be almost as inexplicable as Lear's. Most people can figure out from the story that the young prince is acting erratically on purpose in order to confuse those around him, especially his uncle Claudius. That means that he is following some kind of plan which involves deceiving the other characters. Despite this, many big-name critics, such as Goethe and A.C. Bradley, have applied the *reasoning back to the character of the hero* paradigm to Hamlet and concluded that the explanation for his irrational behaviour is that he is a melancholic procrastinator. The thinking goes something like this:

"I don't understand Hamlet's behaviour; therefore, he must be depressed/ melancholic."

This leads to a second problem with this kind of thinking: it very quickly becomes a catch-all explanation. Whenever Hamlet does something ambiguous, it gets ascribed to an inner emotional state. Whenever Lear does something weird, we just say that's because he is going mad. Once you've accepted the conclusion, all the parts of the story that don't make sense can simply be waved away. Coleridge's use of this reasoning led him astray in relation to Lear. Goethe and Bradley ended up with an incorrect understanding of Hamlet by the same path.

Reasoning back to the character of the hero was one of the core features of the Romantic paradigm that remained the dominant way to interpret Shakespeare for more than a hundred years. One of the first to push back against it was T.S.

Eliot, who made the excellent counter-proposition that the hero's behaviour needs to be understood in relation to the external pressures and opportunities created by the plot of the story rather than emerging entirely from their inner character. The irony is that, because Eliot was unable to see how the events in Hamlet drive the behaviour of the hero, he concluded that the play itself was a flop. He made the exact same leap of reasoning as Coleridge, only rather than give Shakespeare the benefit of artistic licence, Eliot accuses him of artistic failure. The reasoning could be summarised as follows:

"I don't understand Hamlet's behaviour; therefore, the story of Hamlet is a failed work of art."

This is the general problem with the analysis conducted by the intellectual critics of Shakespeare. They are always jumping out of the work itself and back to academic considerations. We have seen Coleridge and Eliot do it. Samuel Johnson also did it. Another famous example is Voltaire, who railed against the increasing popularity of Shakespeare on the basis that he was a "barbarian" who broke the aesthetic rules that govern the creation of stage plays, specifically, by mixing comedy and tragedy. It would not have amused the philosopher to realise that Shakespeare had already poked fun at exactly this kind of intellectual nit-picking. In Act 2, Scene 2 of Hamlet, he has the old philosopher, Polonius, announce the arrival of the acting troupe by proudly demonstrating his understanding of the various genres: "The best actors in the world, either for Tragedy, Comedy, History, Pastoral, Pastoral-Comical, Historical-Pastoral: Tragical-Historical: Tragical-Comical-Historical-Pastoral..." Polonius knows all the "rules", but he doesn't understand the meaning. That, in a nutshell, is the error of the intellectuals who have approached Shakespeare.

This passage just cited from Hamlet demonstrates that Shakespeare had anticipated the errors of interpretation made by critics such as Coleridge, Voltaire, and Eliot. He shows us a philosopher character in the story misinterpreting the events that are going on around him. The same events were then misunderstood by the same kinds of philosophers reading the story in real life! There is a meta meaning at play here that cannot be accidental. Shakespeare knew full well that the philosophical approach would miss the point.

When confronted with ambiguity in the story, the intellectuals have always sought recourse via whatever ideological explanation they fancied. What none of them did was to approach the problem as follows:

"I don't understand Lear's behaviour; therefore, I will redouble my efforts to comprehend him better before passing judgement."

In other words, what none of them did was to seek the answer in the work itself. To do that requires a discipline that has been sorely missing in the interpretation of Shakespeare. But it also requires a model, a method of interpretation. That is what we will present in this book. The proof of that model will be in the pudding. If we are correct, then we will unlock the meanings of Shakespeare's greatest works that have been missed, even by the big names just mentioned.

The truth is that these thinkers were not entirely wrong. The Romantics were correct that the inner states of the hero are of crucial importance, but they neglected the outward-facing aspects. T.S. Eliot was correct to focus attention on the events that the hero must overcome, but he got carried away with a bunch of irrelevant artistic rules. The error of the Romantics was to presuppose that the character of the hero is immutable. The error of Eliot was to presuppose that the hero has no agency of his own.

The irony is that this dichotomy between the inner world of the hero and the circumstances in which they find themselves plays a central and explicit role in all of Shakespeare's works. "The fault, dear Brutus, is not in our stars but in ourselves..." Shakespeare returns to this theme time and time again. His stories feature a rhythmic flux that alternates between the inner and outer worlds. The identity of his heroes is not fixed and static but dynamic. It is formed and created via an open-ended process, a transformation that ebbs and flows between microcosm (hero) and macrocosm (world). All of Shakespeare's stories are predicated on this tension.

The hero of every Shakespeare story is going through a process where their identity is undone and then recreated. What differentiates Shakespeare's heroes is the degree to which they consciously and deliberately attempt to navigate that process, to create their own identity. That is something very different from the philosophy of old, which required submission to rules. Thus, the argument between Shakespeare and the philosophers is not accidental or limited to textual interpretation; it boils down to a disagreement about some of the fundamental aspects of reality and human existence.

Whereas ideology only views the world through a narrow prism, Shakespeare enlarges our world because he shows the process of becoming to a degree of intensity and intricacy that is still unparalleled. That is why it is worth our time and trouble to understand him. That is why we cannot leave the job to ideologues and art critic nit-pickers.

What we will do in this book is interpret Shakespeare on his own terms, reading nothing into his works but what is already there. What we will find is an expression of that aspect of human existence that the philosophers had explicitly ignored. It is the nature of becoming, transformation and change. It is what we will call the *journey into the sacred.*

Identity and Transformation

It is perfectly possible to read or watch a Shakespeare play and get a great deal out of it without knowing any fancy theories about how it all works. The Bard was popular with all segments of Elizabethan society, including the uneducated common folk of the era. His stories remain known by practically everybody in our time. Their general appeal has not waned, and the universality of their themes should ensure their popularity for a very long time to come. It is nevertheless true that the general understanding of the works is either partial or often just plain wrong. As we have already intimated, this is true of King Lear and Hamlet. It is also true of The Tempest and Othello as well. We might be tempted to say that these works have hidden meanings. But the meanings are not really hidden. What is missing is our own understanding. To see them, we have to change the way we think about Shakespeare.

Therefore, before we get into our analysis of the stories themselves, we need to lay the groundwork for our method of reading Shakespeare. Most of this method is applicable to any great work of art that is based in storytelling. But, as we will see, it is also applicable to any story at all, including the ones we tell in everyday life. It turns out that there is an underlying structure that is general to all stories, from the ones we tell our friends at the pub on a Friday evening to the greatest works of literature.

It might be objected that Shakespeare was more than a writer of stories. He was a writer of plays, and those plays were intended to be performed on stage, where a whole host of other forms of artistic expression were employed, such as acting, diction, costume, scenery, etc. Furthermore, it is undeniable that the Bard was a master at various literary techniques such as rhyme and meter, metaphor, conceit, and allegory. By focusing on the stories alone, aren't we ignoring these other modes of expression? The answer is, yes, but it is a yes that is made with full consciousness. Nothing that we discuss in this book negates all the finer qualities of Shakespeare's work, and the fact that all those qualities exist on top of the themes we will explore is testament to Shakespeare's genius. However, it is still the case that the core meanings of the works are to be found in the stories and that the misinterpretations that have occurred can only be corrected by an analysis of those stories.

What we must do first of all, then, is re-evaluate our understanding of a concept that is so ubiquitous that most people have probably never stopped to think about it. We must retune our understanding of the meaning of a "story". As a first step, let's conduct a very brief summary of the intellectual history of those who have already undertaken the task.

Aristotle is our starting point. His work *Poetics* set out primarily to investigate the art form of Greek tragedy. Since tragedy included all kinds of other elements, including music, the philosopher needed to incorporate these into his analysis. He identified six primary criteria. The first of those was the one that Aristotle believed was most important. It gets translated into modern English using a term that everybody would be familiar with – "plot". However, the actual word that Aristotle used was "mythos", and "mythos" was the Greek word for "story". In other words, two and a half millennia ago, Aristotle had already acknowledged that the most important element in Greek tragedy was the story. That's where he focused his attention, just as we will do in relation to Shakespeare.

A second important semantic point is that the title of Aristotle's work came from the Greek word "poiesis", which meant "to make". The word could be applied to handcrafts or any other kind of production. When applied to stories, the connotation was that the stories were "made up", implying a difference from the stories we tell in everyday life, which are mostly based on real events. The great Greek tragedians were professionals who spent a great deal of time and effort on their works and were rewarded for their efforts. Clearly, there is a skill to creating a great (fictional) story. Nevertheless, it is also true that the structure of the greatest story is the same as the kind we tell in everyday life. This is a key point to which we will return later.

Beginning with Aristotle, we get two key properties of stories that are still used in our time. There is plot (*mythos*) and character (*ethos*). The former relates to the events that occur and the latter to the nature of the characters. It would be more than two millennia before any meaningful improvement would be made on this scheme, and, although there were other important thinkers that contributed, we will skip straight to the man whose work will inform our analysis here, Joseph Campbell. Campbell was a comparative mythologist who conducted exhaustive studies of myths from around the world and arrived at an underlying structure that appears to be universal. He called it the *hero's journey*.

Before we outline Campbell's innovations, we must remark on an incredible semantic "coincidence". We have seen that Aristotle foregrounded the *mythos* of the work of art, i.e., the story. In modern English, the word "myth" is now applied to a specific kind of story, one that usually features supernatural elements and which is assumed to be somehow foundational to the culture from which it arises. This mode of interpretation grew out of the heady mix of historical, anthropological, archaeological, and psychoanalytic scholarship that exploded in the 19th and earlier 20th centuries. Campbell's work was arguably the greatest product of that milieu. However, because he was working within a "mythical" paradigm with overt influences from psychoanalysis, his concept of the hero's journey has always had a quasi-mystical tinge. Furthermore, because modern literature at that time had begun to move away from telling stories, the hero's journey idea was not seen to be applicable to contemporary works. For these reasons and more, it seems not to have occurred to anybody that what Campbell had discovered was the universal structure of all stories, not just what we now call myths.

From this very brief overview, we can see why the concept of a *story* has not received the attention it deserves. Aristotle was studying Greek tragedy. Campbell was studying mythology. The modern discipline of literature studied only written works. Anthropology was more concerned with spoken stories. History had been split off into its own discipline, as had folklore, psychology, and others. With scholars working in so many nominally unrelated fields, nobody realised that the underlying structure of the stories they were examining was the same. It's the same structure that we find in the works of Shakespeare and the stories we tell about our own lives. That is the re-evaluation that we must make. We must learn to see the features that are shared by all stories. The reason to do so is not to score points in some academic competition but to unlock the deeper meanings in Shakespeare and other great works of art, which in turn unlocks some core truths of human existence.

Aristotle gave us plot and character, which we may think of as the hero of the story and the events the hero goes through. Nevertheless, Aristotle saw the events themselves as being the key feature. Campbell's great advance was to realise that a story is fundamentally about the hero. What is really going on in every story is a transformation of the hero. The events of the story get their meaning from the manner in which they describe that transformation. Therefore, to understand stories, we must understand the nature of transformation.

Because Campbell's approach was made within the discipline of mythology, and because he had an explicitly psychoanalytic focus, he emphasised the inner or spiritual transformation of the hero. That is valid. But we must expand our definition to include all the ways in which the hero may be transformed, including their outer, social identity, their opinions, their worldview, and all the other factors that go into making us human. When we do that, we get the following definition of a story that we will use in this book:

A story is the process by which the hero's identity is transformed.

Sounds simple, doesn't it? In fact, there is a great deal of complexity in the two concepts of "identity" and "transformation". We will need to spend the rest of this chapter unpacking them both.

Before we do that, there is one final point to make. Aristotle famously said that art imitates life. He meant this primarily in relation to the superficial elements such as the behaviour of the actors, their costume, mannerisms, etc. The truth is much more fundamental. Stories imitate life because life is itself a series of transformations. Each transformation that we go through changes our identity in some way. That is true for major turning points such as puberty, marriage, our first job, etc. But it is true even at the everyday level. Every time we tell a story about something that happened to us, we are telling the story of a transformation we have experienced. Art imitates life because life is transformation. What is being transformed is always the identity of the hero. Therefore, to understand stories, we must first be clear about the meaning of identity.

A Map of Identity

Most people are familiar with the thought experiment, "If a tree falls in the forest and nobody is around, does it make a sound?" We may ask a similar question in relation to stories: "If a transformation happens but nobody talks about it, is it a story?" Although a little clumsy, this formulation allows us to make clear why thinkers since the time of Plato and Aristotle have taken an interest in art but not in the everyday kinds of stories we tell each other. The difference lies in the magnitude of the transformation. Everyday stories are always about small transformations for the simple reason that we are limited in the amount of time we have to tell them. The larger a transformation is, the more complex it is, and therefore the more time it takes to tell. Only skilled storytellers are capable of handling the complexity involved in larger transformations. For that reason, everyday people don't tell stories about the larger and more complex transformations in their lives. To answer the thought experiment: the transformation still occurred, but nobody told a story about it.

It follows from this that stories about the larger transformations of life have been left to various skilled storytellers down through the ages, including poets, muses, authors, playwrights, troubadours, bards, etc. Even though the stories created by these practitioners are usually fictional, the transformations themselves are still "real" in the sense that they map to those we go through that we go through in our own lives. That is one of the main reasons why such stories resonate so strongly with us. They express something that we can't express for ourselves.

What is being transformed in every story is the identity of the hero. While identity has countless specific details, of all which constitute the individuality of any one of us, it is also true that life has a set of phases with relatively fixed transitions between them. These phases make up the major identity transformations that art so often deals with.

We already have a useful shorthand to denote these common identity transformations thanks to the work of Carl Jung and the closely related scholarship of psychoanalyst Erik Erikson. Jung noted that what he called the *archetypes* were prevalent in all kinds of stories, from ancient myths to modern film and everything in between. One of Erikson's innovations was to realise that the archetypes denote phases of life. When we put the two together, we get a map of the common identity transformations over the whole human lifespan.

We begin with the archetypes Child, Orphan, Adult, and Elder. The simplest way to understand these is by biological criteria. Puberty is the transition between the Child and Orphan. Maturity denotes the Adult archetype and senescence the Elder. Each of these biological transitions coincides more or less exactly with a wider transformation of identity. For example, puberty ushers in sexual maturity, and this changes our relationships with our family, friends, and wider society. Because puberty is the time when the intellectual faculties are awakened, what used to be called the *age of reason*, it is also when we are first initiated into our culture in a more rigorous and sophisticated fashion than was the case during childhood, where education is mostly about mimicry and rote learning. We can construct a similar set of broad properties for the transformations to Adult and Elder respectively.

Now it might be argued that we could just use the everyday terms *childhood, adolescence, adulthood*, and *old age* to denote these life phases. However, our analysis will require us to be more precise, and so we will use the archetype as a symbol that denotes a number of general properties that we innately understand. This fits with Jung's idea of the archetypes as belonging to what he called the *collective unconscious*. We draw on this innate knowledge without consciously thinking about it. That is why the archetypes are so useful in storytelling because they communicate a great deal of information without the author needing to spell it out. By bringing these concepts to consciousness, we open up parts of our understanding that are normally hidden, and this allows for greater awareness in interpretation.

The archetypes allow us to understand the broad developmental changes we go through over the course of life. We can further enhance our map by adding four broad categories of identity. These are the biological-familial, the economic, the political, and the religious. The first relates to the parts of our identity pertaining to family membership, including the genetic traits that define our appearance, our interpersonal relationships within the family, the wealth and resources that are shared, etc. The other three categories are about the identity we form from interactions with wider society. Our economic identity is whatever role defines our productive contribution to the larger group. Political identity is our place in the exercise of power and decision-making. Religious identity relates to the ceremonies and beliefs that constitute the worldview that we are initiated into.

These categories of identity intersect with the archetypes in predictable ways. For example, seemingly all societies leave the Child in the care of its family for about the first half dozen years of life. During this time, the Child has no independent identity in the economic, political, and religious domains. That changes with the onset of the Orphan archetype where we are given responsibility in those domains for the first time. The Adult phase of life represents maturity in the biological sphere and also the others as we attain a peak of performance. The Elder phase then represents an easing off of activity and a transition to a mentor or leadership role in accordance with the experience accumulated throughout the course of life. These general patterns hold for everybody, although there are countless variations across individuals and cultures.

We have now defined the four archetypes and the four categories of identity. The final concept we need deals with the distinction between the inner and outer-facing poles of existence. We will refer to the former as the esoteric and the latter as the exoteric.

Our exoteric identity refers to those aspects that can be seen from a third-person point of view. Each of the four categories of identity has an exoteric pole. In relation to the biological-familial, the most obvious are the physical attributes we inherit genetically, such as eye, skin, and hair colour, height, body type, etc. The exoteric aspects of our economic, political, and religious identities refer to any special clothing, forms of address and language, or ceremonial and ritual participation that mark us out as belonging to various institutions in those domains.

By contrast, the esoteric pole of identity pertains to the inner, subjective experiences of life. In the biological realm, this includes states such as hunger, thirst, arousal, tiredness, sleepiness, etc. In the economic sphere, we may be disillusioned with our work or highly motivated towards it. We may feel that our political institutions are corrupt and decadent or we may trust and respect them. In relation to religious matters, we may experience the wonders of spiritual bliss or the terror of despair. More broadly, the esoteric domain of identity includes our thoughts, feelings, desires, emotions, worldview, opinions, beliefs, and more.

When we put all this together, we obtain a map of identity that incorporates the major transformations that occur throughout the course of life. Firstly, there is the Child-to-Orphan transformation which includes puberty in the biological sphere and the beginning of an economic, political, and religious identity via initiation into the institutions of society associated with each domain. The Orphan-to-Adult transformation is most strongly associated with marriage, which represents the continuation of the family line. In the other domains, this represents the time in which we achieve full membership in the institutions that we are now a member of. Finally, the Adult-to-Elder transition maps to becoming a grandparent in the familial sphere and the transition to a mentor or teaching role in the other domains. In the modern world, there is also the notion of retirement at this time of life. It is no coincidence that each of these transitions appears so commonly in fictional stories that there is a genre for them. The Child-to-Orphan transition are known as coming-of-age stories. Love and marriage are captured by the genre of love stories. It is noteworthy that the Adult-to-Elder does not have its own genre, although the Elder archetype appears in stories that feature Orphan heroes.

The final set of archetypes we need to cover also appears in countless stories. These can be thought of as sub-archetypes of the Adult phase of life. There are the Father, Mother, Warrior, Ruler, and Sage. Note that each of these maps to one of the categories of identity we have defined. The Father and Mother belong to the familial domain. The Warrior belongs to the economic, the Ruler to the political, and the Sage to the religious. The nature of these should be fairly self-evident, but it is worth noting that a specific transformation is required to transition into each archetype. In relation to the Father and Mother, pregnancy-childbirth is the transformation that leads the individual into the role. The Warrior must be initiated into the martial arts, which, in the modern military, is done via boot camp. For the Ruler, there are whatever trials are required to earn the political position, e.g., a democratic election. For the Sage, there is the period of education and training that signifies membership into the leadership role of the religion or worldview being practised.

Each archetype also has a number of common transformations that are well understood in the general culture. For the Father and Mother, these are mostly related to child-rearing, with the sickness of the Child being the most common. Warriors are called on to go to war. Rulers must make difficult decisions with unknown outcomes. Sages deal with the bigger questions of life and provide guidance to others navigating those questions. All of these issues are dealt with in fictional stories that feature these archetypes, but we must once again stress that the transformations themselves are very much based in the lived experience of people who have those roles in real life. The archetypes are real, not merely imaginary.

In relation to our understanding of Shakespeare, the benefits of this largely abstract model of identity come from the counterintuitive fact that the Bard is the ultimate portraitist of individuality. His characters are memorable because of their uniqueness. However, as we will see, all of his greatest stories feature heroes who are going through the exact archetypal transformations we have just listed. Romeo and Juliet are trying to get married. Othello and

Desdemona have just been married. Macbeth is a Warrior who has just fought a war. King Lear is trying to step back from his role as Ruler and make the transition to Elder. The circumstances of these heroes are unique, but the broader situation they find themselves in is common. By understanding the more general nature of their circumstances, we deepen our appreciation for the transformation they are going through. Paradoxically, by understanding what is universal about Shakespeare's heroes, we appreciate them more as individuals.

Now that we have our basic map of identity, the last element we need before beginning our analysis proper is to unpack the concept of "transformation".

The Nature of Transformation

Let's imagine a very common kind of identity transformation that can occur in the modern world. The hero of our story is going to get a job. We'll raise the stakes slightly by making it her first job. Let's call our hero Mary. She is in her mid-teens and still in school. With the blessing of her parents, Mary has decided to start looking for casual work to earn some pocket money. Although we don't think about it in these terms in real life, Mary has decided to change her identity. In order to understand any change, we must first understand the starting state. To do that, we can employ the map of identity just outlined.

Mary begins in the stable identity which we have called the Child archetype. She is in the care of her parents, but she is also dependent on them. If Mary wants something, she has to ask her father or mother to buy it for her or to give her the money to do so. The positive side of the Child is that there are no responsibilities to worry about. The negative side is that you have to do what you're told. This is why Mary's decision to find a job signifies a much larger transformation than might appear to be the case on first glance. It is not just about money or work, it is about independence. The trade-off for independence is responsibility. That is a core feature of what we have called the Orphan archetype. Therefore, the decision to find a job actually represents part of Mary's transition from Child to Orphan.

What does that transition look like in practice? We all know the steps required to get a job. Mary leaves the safety and security of the family home and ventures into the world by looking for available positions and then interviewing for them. She will have to meet new people who will be judging her as a suitable candidate or not. She needs to be aware of how she is presenting herself in dress, speech, and manner. She needs to learn a new set of behaviours that are appropriate to the context in which she finds herself.

During this time, Mary is striving after the identity of *employee*. As anybody who has gone through a period of unemployment knows, this can be very challenging. Being rejected is always a difficult thing in life, but it's even harder when you are uncertain about your identity in the first place. If Mary doesn't have much support from her family and friends, it is easy to imagine her becoming dejected in her job search and perhaps even giving up altogether. That can have major ramifications for her future success, not just in the job market but in life in general. This raises one of the key properties of the transformation process. To leave behind an identity and try to forge a new one always entails an amount of risk leading to outcomes that are unforeseeable and unknowable in advance. Nevertheless, it is true that the risk is lower for identity transformations that are well known and established. It is unlikely, although not impossible, that Mary's job search will end in disaster.

If we imagine that Mary does succeed in finding a job, the final stage of the transformation is the time after she has nominally secured the new identity. This can also be a difficult period because, up until now, Mary has only believed that she wanted to become an employee. Until she actually experiences what it is like to be one, she doesn't know whether it is something that she really wants. That is why the first few weeks on the job are crucial, not just for Mary to figure out whether the situation suits her, but also for her employer to be sure she is capable of the role. She also needs to settle into the wider work environment, get along with her colleagues, etc.

If all that goes well, then we can say that Mary has transitioned into the role of *employee*. This is a change not just in her exoteric identity but her esoteric one too. She may experience the newfound confidence that comes with growing her skills and making new friends. The money she makes gives her a measure of independence from her parents, and this can flow through to other changes of outlook. There may be all kinds of other smaller changes and effects, both good and bad, that Mary needs to work through. One thing is for sure, a transformation has taken place.

With this brief summary, which could easily be a real-life story or one that forms the basis of a film or young adult novel (almost certainly with a love interest thrown in to spice it up), we have described not just the surface details of Mary's journey to becoming an employee, we have also related the underlying structure that sits beneath all transformations and stories. The hero of the story always begins in what we will call *holy state.* The word *holy* is etymologically related to the words *whole* and *healthy.* When we refer to holy state, we are talking about the hero's identity when it is secure, comfortable, and stable. This is true both in the exoteric sense that society recognises the identity and in the esoteric sense that the hero has no wish to change it. Mary begins as a Child and we presume that she, her parents, and her wider family are perfectly okay with that situation. That is the holy state.

Next comes the trigger that will move the hero into what we will call *sacred state.* The word *sacred* simply means to make holy. When we are in sacred state, we are trying to get back to holy state. Sacred state denotes a midway point where the hero is striving towards a new identity that they have not yet attained. Mary wants to get a job. Until she gets one, she is in sacred state. The sacred part of her transformation includes all the actions and emotions that come with trying to attain that goal, including the mental and logistical preparation for interviews, any setbacks along the way, discussions with family and friends about the matter, and anything at all that relates to the end state she is moving towards.

The transition from holy state to sacred state requires a sacrifice. Some part of the old identity has to be relinquished. In relation to Mary, we might say that, as a teenager who is not relying on work to survive, she doesn't have anything to lose and therefore nothing to sacrifice. After all, if she doesn't find a job, she can continue to live at home, go to school, and do whatever else she used to do. That may be true, but there are a number of other things Mary is sacrificing. At the most basic level, she must sacrifice the time and energy it takes to look for jobs, to apply for them, to travel to interviews, etc.

She must give up doing whatever she used to do during that time and turn her attention towards a new goal. That is the immediate sacrifice that must be made.

More abstractly, but no less importantly, Mary is sacrificing the comfort and ease of life as a dependent Child. By putting herself in situations where others will judge her, she risks her self-esteem and self-confidence. That can spill over into all kinds of other problems that may affect her schooling and relationships with her family. This is tied to the criteria of risk that is an inevitable part of any transformation. Risk implies a potential sacrifice that can only truly be known once it manifests.

All of this holds for the scenario where the hero has initiated their own transformation. In the story of Mary, we have assumed that she instigated the search for work based on her own internal motivations and desires. That doesn't mean Mary will be fully aware of the sacrifices that are required of her, but it does mean she is approaching the issue with a high degree of conscious will. However, transformations do not always begin in this fashion. Sometimes, the hero of a story may be thrown into the process unexpectedly. They are still required to make a sacrifice, they just didn't see it coming. In that case, we might prefer to use the phrase *identity crisis* to refer to the event which triggers the transformation.

The word "crisis" comes from the Greek, where it simply means "time for a decision". We normally think of a crisis as originating from external factors rather than internal motivations. We can easily adapt Mary's story to reflect this change of focus. Let's imagine she is a little bit older. She has just finished her schooling. Rather than seek work willingly, it is left to her parents to pressure her into it. Perhaps her parents have been hinting at what is required for some time, but Mary hasn't gotten the message. Finally, an ultimatum is given: get a job or face the consequences. Mary has now been thrust into an identity crisis. She still has to make a decision one way or another, and the decision still implies a sacrifice, it's just that the impetus for it comes from her parents. It is an exoteric trigger rather than an esoteric one.

Remember that the sacred state means that the hero's identity has become un-whole or split. With the ultimatum from her parents, not only has Mary's economic identity been called into question, her family identity is also under challenge. Until the matter is resolved one way or another, she will be in sacred state.

In truth, almost every transformation is partly driven by a combination of internal and external factors, and therefore the transition out of holy state and into sacred implies both a sacrifice and an identity crisis. The sacred state ends and the hero transitions back to holy state once the new identity is as secure and comfortable as the original one at the start of the transformation. This does not mean that the hero attains the goal they expected. It is in the nature of the sacred, and the transformation process more broadly, that there is an irreducible element of uncertainty involved. The journey into the sacred always involves risk, unpredictability, and ambiguity. That is why the outcome can never be known in advance. Mary may get rejected from two or three jobs and fall into a crippling depression that takes months or years to get out of. Alternatively, she may land a job with an upcoming business tycoon who takes her on as a mentee. She may quickly climb through the ranks of the company and end up as CEO within short order. When we step into the sacred, anything is possible.

Thus, every transformation involves a transition from a holy state where the hero's identity is whole and known into sacred state where there is uncertainty and ambiguity and back to a known holy state at the end where a new identity has been attained. We may summarise the nature of transformation in diagram form as follows:-

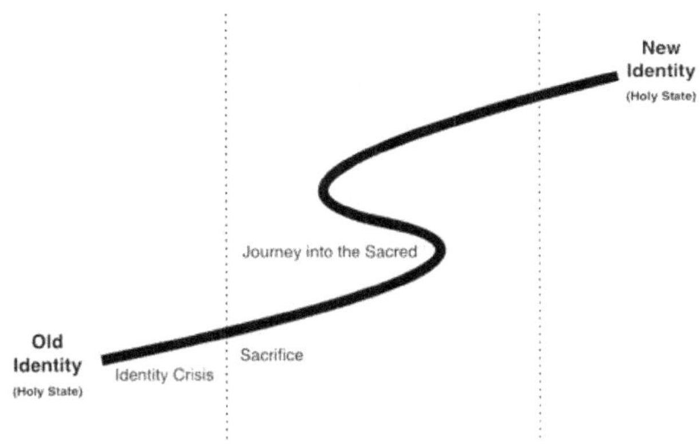

Every transformation and every story involves the hero sacrificing their old identity and striving towards the new. This process may intersect with any components in our map of identity. Thus, there we can think of the transformation in terms of the archetype of the hero, as we did with Mary's transition from Child to Orphan. We may think of it in terms of the four categories of identity, with Mary's economic identity being the primary element in her story. Finally, we may think of it in terms of the exoteric and esoteric poles of existence, as in Mary obtaining the official title of employee at whichever company she ends up working for and then Mary's internal responses to this in terms of emotions, feelings, intellectual growth, and perhaps even change of worldview as she comes to directly experience a new kind of identity.

We must remember that our model of identity is just a map and we must not confuse the map for the territory. Every person is a unique individual in unique circumstances. Although useful for analytical purposes, real life does not necessarily fit into neat categories. Mary's attempted transformation into the economic identity of employee will have ramifications on her familial identity, potentially also her identity as a student, her friendships, and other areas of her life. More broadly, every transformation throws our entire equilibrium into uncertainty. That is one reason why the sacred state always has risk associated with it. The purpose of our map is to provide a heuristic to guide understanding. Its validity will be proven shortly when we put it to work to unpack the stories of Shakespeare.

As a final point, we need to address what might appear to be a contradiction in our model. We have said that every transformation ends in holy state, but we also said that the sacred state is inherently irrational and unpredictable. If that's true, then we can't know the outcome of any transformation. What is to stop the hero getting stuck in sacred state? In fact, that is what we see in all of Shakespeare's tragedies. The hero does not attain the holy state they were striving for. That is true of Hamlet, Macbeth, Lear, and others. Doesn't this mean our model of transformation is wrong?

Life is made up of countless transformation cycles. Most of them are of small magnitude. The power of the archetype concept is that it denotes transformations that are both major and universal. Puberty is a major transformation, as are marriage, pregnancy, and childbirth. For most people, getting their first job is a major event that changes their orientation to the world and to themselves. The power of Shakespeare is that he constructs for his heroes transformations that go beyond the norm. The magnitude of their identity crisis and sacrifice is massively heightened as a result.

Thus far, we have concentrated entirely on the transformations that can occur during life. We have not addressed the transformation that begins life or the one that ends it. Birth is the transformation that begets all the others. Death is the transformation that ends all others. Therein lies the answer to our question of whether it is possible to "get stuck" in sacred state and never complete a transformation. The answer is no. Every transformation must eventually end in death. That is exactly what happens to Lear, Macbeth, and Hamlet. They may not attain the holy state that they were seeking, but their transformation was ended with their lives. Therefore, the question of whether a transformation must end in holy state resolves back to a theological problem: is death a holy state?

Every religion, in one form or another, answers this question in the affirmative, although many construct elaborate means by which the final holy state may be achieved, and some deny that the holy state will be attained by certain people, who will spend the rest of eternity stuck in sacred state. Since the greatest storytellers invariably deal with the question of death, it follows that they also must provide an answer to this question, not directly but through the way in which they represent the meaning of death. Shakespeare is no exception. His tragedies communicate his understanding of the meaning of death and therefore also about the meaning of life. They do so precisely because the hero does not attain the holy state they sought after. They are returned to a higher, more universal holy state.

This is another reason why Shakespeare's works are the equal of any philosophy or theology: they deal with the fundamental questions of human existence. It is also why it is crucial for us to have an understanding of transformation in order to unlock these higher truths. The theoretical model we have just outlined is inevitably rather dry and bland. It is technically necessary in order to grasp the meanings of stories and transformations, but there is something far more profound at play. The question of transformation brings us face-to-face with the nature of existence.

Every transformation and every story involves the hero sacrificing some part of their old identity and striving towards the new. The journey into the sacred is always irrational, not just in the sense that it throws us back onto the non-rational parts of our being but also in that a transformation is a novel and evolving process where the parameters that we thought we understood are themselves changing. What the hero thinks they are sacrificing at the start of the story and what they ultimately end up sacrificing are not the same thing. Not only can the destination come as a surprise, we may realise later that we didn't even know where we were starting from. That is why, four hundred years after his death, we can still find new meanings in the great works of Shakespeare. Let's do that now.

Much Ado About Nothing

A story is about the transformation of the hero. In the simple kinds of stories we tell in everyday settings, there is almost always a single hero: ourselves. In great works of literature, however, there are many characters, each of whom is going through their own journey of transformation. Such works are made up of multiple intersecting stories in much the same way that counterpoint works in musical composition. But it's also true to say that there is a main theme. The stories of the lesser characters are subordinate to and contained within the trajectory of the primary hero. This is true in King Lear, Macbeth, and Hamlet, to name just a few.

There is no rule, however, to say that there always must be one primary hero. In fact, Shakespeare gives us several stories featuring two or more. Where he presents us with dual heroes of equal billing, it is almost always a love story, the most famous of which is Romeo and Juliet. In such cases, even though there are two heroes, they are both pursuing the same transformation (love, marriage), and so their stories are fundamentally linked. In Much Ado About Nothing, Shakespeare gives us four heroes divided into pairs of lovers whose stories are also interlinked.

This facilitates a common pattern we will see throughout our analysis where the Bard provides us with multiple perspectives on the same underlying dynamic. In *Much Ado*, he wants us to compare and contrast between the two sets of lovers as we watch four heroes go through the same transformation. There is the younger couple, Claudio and Hero, and the more experienced one, Benedick and Beatrice.

For Shakespeare, the holy state at the end of a love story is always marriage.

The sacred state that precedes marriage is love itself. Since ancient times and through the Renaissance, love had been seen as a dangerous emotion capable of tearing families apart and causing war and destruction. That is why love belongs to the sacred state where many things may go wrong. Shakespeare would show us in Romeo and Juliet how love could lead to tragedy. But Much Ado About Nothing is a comedy, and that means the outcome will be a happy one for the heroes of the story.

In some respects, the love story is the simplest of all stories. A couple meet and fall head over heels for each other. What could be simpler? Possibly because of this simplicity, love stories can reveal important changes in culture over time. Our modern love stories focus almost entirely on the esoteric journey that the lovers go through. For us, love is an inherently internal state. The transformation of the heroes in a modern love story is largely psychological for this reason. Marriage is an optional extra. We focus on the esoteric journey.

Although Shakespeare marks a major turning point leading towards our modern esoteric conception of love, his era still very much had an understanding of love as including exoteric notions such as duty and honour. It was precisely these virtues that were seen to be placed under threat whenever esoteric love appeared on the scene. Thus, the classical love story involves a rift between the exoteric and esoteric aspects of the hero's identity that is perfectly in keeping with our notion of the sacred. In pursuing their esoteric romance, the lovers had to break their exoteric commitments of duty and honour to family and society, thereby causing a split in their identities and thrusting them into sacred state.

This is an issue that arises in almost every one of Shakespeare's stories that we will cover in this book, and it is one of the general differences between our time and his that we need to factor in. In Elizabethan England, and certainly in the ancient world of Greece and Rome, honour was something to be maintained at all costs. In our terminology, honour is our exoteric identity. It is the way we are perceived by society. Honour is built and maintained from our behaviour, not necessarily from our thoughts and feelings, since we may learn to keep these secret from the outer world. A slight on one's honour was a very serious matter for the people of Shakespeare's time. For men, the primary recourse was to challenge the culprit to a duel. Women had to rely on their father and brothers to avenge their honour. If those family members refused to do so, because they believed the woman really had overstepped the bounds of propriety, the woman would find herself in a very difficult situation. Shakespeare incorporates both of these themes into Much Ado About Nothing.

There is a reason why Shakespeare is so important not just as a great storyteller in his own right but as a harbinger for the cultural changes that still dominate in our time. The classical and Renaissance love story played out almost entirely in the exoteric domain, where honour was restored one way or another, usually at the pointy end of a sword. Although Shakespeare does not deny the validity of the exoteric, his focus is always on the inner, esoteric dimensions of his heroes. That is true in Much Ado About Nothing and all his other works. In this respect, we may say that Shakespeare is the creator of the modern love story, and Much Ado About Nothing is one of his most important contributions to that effect.

Having identified the four heroes, our first step in understanding the story is to define their starting holy state. The story begins in the luxurious estate of local governor Leonato. It is a paragon of Renaissance-era refinement featuring beautiful people playing games, singing and dancing, and otherwise having a great time. Among the beautiful people are Leonato's daughter, Hero, and his niece, Beatrice. A messenger brings news that a great friend of the family, Don Pedro, will be stopping by on his return from fighting a victorious military campaign abroad. Don Pedro's letter contains news of a gallant young man who played a crucial role in the victory, Claudio. Meanwhile, Beatrice takes the opportunity to enquire after another man known to the family called Benedick. We learn that he too will be joining the party that is set to arrive at any minute.

A more charming introduction to a story is hard to imagine. We are among prosperous, accomplished, and eloquent people who demonstrate the art of living well. Don Pedro's party arrives, and many pleasant words are spoken. All of this belongs to the holy state of the story. We have old friends reuniting for an extended stay that promises to be a delight for all concerned. But the holy state also includes the starting identity for each character, an identity in which they are comfortable and competent. Thus, we see Beatrice and Benedick resume their love-hate relationship. They are an older and more experienced couple. We find that both have sworn off love altogether. At least, that is what they desperately want everybody to believe. Don Pedro is in his element visiting his old friend Leonato and showing off his protégé, Claudio. Hero is at ease in her own home with her best friend and cousin Beatrice by her side. All of this belongs to the holy state that is the start of every story.

The first crack in the holy state comes at the end of Scene 1 when we find out that, despite the fact that not a single word passed between them, Claudio has fallen instantly in love with Hero. He turns to his mentor for advice, and Don Pedro promises to arrange the marriage for him by wooing Hero on his behalf at the masquerade ball that will take place that evening. This is a rather deceptive and inappropriate-sounding scheme, but Don Pedro's extremely close relationship with Leonato means we have every reason to expect that the marriage is as good as a foregone conclusion. Thus, the holy state persists, although Claudio has taken a tentative step into the sacred by falling in love.

All of this sets up the transformation for both Claudio and Hero. These are two young people who are at the age where getting married is to be expected. Given that they are a perfect match in terms of their social standing and the fact that they fall for each other instantly, there is nothing at all stopping their marriage. In fact, the holy state for Claudio and Hero is so holy that it would have already been a total cliché for Elizabethan audiences. Love-at-first-sight stories were a dime a dozen. Where Shakespeare gets innovative is in the second couple, and it is no coincidence that the innovation rests on a sophisticated backstory that is a feature of his best works. This introduces a technique that will be crucial for our understanding of all Shakespeare's works. Since an understanding of it will be necessary moving forward, we need to spend a moment now to introduce it.

Some readers would have heard of the concept of "exposition". This refers to the way in which the author fills in the backstory to the main story as it is presented . A very common way to handle exposition is via spoken or written narration. Think of Star Wars and the "long time ago in a galaxy far, far away" introductory sequence. That is written exposition which gives us the context for the story we are about to witness. Another method of exposition is to have one or more of the characters tell us the backstory via dialogue. Finally, we may be given access to the inner thoughts of a character to learn about the broader context. We will call these standard techniques "overt exposition". There is nothing subtle about them. In fact, they are impossible to miss.

Shakespeare does make use of overt exposition, but the far more important technique we need to understand his work is what we will call "covert exposition". As the name suggests, this is a way of filling in the backstory by implication. Shakespeare was a true master of this technique and was able to create incredibly intricate backstories for his characters with very little overt description or dialogue. But it's even more brilliant than that. Remember that every story features a transition from holy state to sacred state. The purpose of exposition is to flesh out the holy state that the hero was in before the identity crisis that signals the transition to sacred state. Because Shakespeare is able to create detailed exposition via implication, he is able to push the holy state back into the time before the action begins. This allows him to begin the action of the story with an almost immediate transition to sacred state. In fact, in the case of Hamlet and Lear, the hero is already in sacred state when we meet them. To fully understand the story, therefore, we must be able to fill in the implied holy state that Shakespeare creates via his technique of covert exposition. The failure to do this sits at the heart of most of the misinterpretation of the Bard's work that has occurred over the centuries. It's for this reason that much of our analysis in this book will involve unpacking the covert exposition of the story.

Much Ado About Nothing provides us with a very gentle way to ease ourselves into the practice of deciphering covert exposition because the backstory of Benedick and Beatrice is fairly straightforward. They were once in love but, for some reason, were not able to consummate it. That is what lies behind the charming verbal jousting that goes on between the two and their unusual attitudes towards love and marriage. Importantly, what that signifies is that their holy state lies well before the beginning of the story. Despite the fact that the overall atmosphere at the start of the play is very much indicative of holy state, Benedick and Beatrice are really in sacred state with their relationship unresolved.

On the surface of it, Benedick and Beatrice are an inversion of Claudio and Hero since they seem to hate each other and have explicitly sworn off ideas of marriage and love altogether. But we and the other characters can easily see that both of them are overcompensating. This love-hate relationship has become so common in stories and films in the modern world that we forgot how novel it was in Shakespeare's time. The love-at-first-sight pattern of Claudio and Hero was the normal one for love stories in the Elizabethan era. Shakespeare gives us that cliché and then explicitly contrasts it with something more complex, interesting, and novel. He leads us to believe that the love between Claudio and Hero is a foregone conclusion. That frees us up to wonder what is going on between Beatrice and Benedick. Their transformation is where the interest lies.

The implication is that Beatrice and Benedick used to be just like Claudio and Hero, but something went wrong. Rather than end in tragedy or depression, both of them have turned this failure into a part of their identity by swearing off love altogether. We might argue that this identity is stable and secure, and therefore they really are in holy state when the story begins. It is also important that the two of them have created this identity for themselves, and that makes them more sophisticated and individualistic than the other characters in the story. That is a big part of the reason why we cannot know what is going to happen with them. The brilliant part about this is that we know that every story requires a sacrifice from the hero(es). What Beatrice and Benedick will have to sacrifice is their overt cynicism about love and marriage. That is not going to be a trivial matter because both have made it central to their identity.

Thus, the holy state at the beginning of the action sets up two parallel love stories, one of which is a complete cliché and one of which is novel. As if that weren't good enough, the novel story will rescue the clichéd one from itself in just the same way that the novel heroes, Beatrice and Benedick, will help save the clichéd ones, Claudio and Hero. Because the love-hate story has become cliché in our own time, it is difficult for us to realise why it was so innovative to the Elizabethans. In order to grasp that, we need to factor in the cultural background.

Our approach to Shakespeare in this book will have three main layers. The universal layer is what we denote by the archetypes, our map of identity, and our understanding that every story is a transformation. On top of that, there is a layer of culture. Finally, there is the hero in their individuality. We won't be spending much time on the last of these for the simple reason that there can be no better way to understand the individuality of the characters than by reading the works themselves or watching the plays. Any description we could give here would be nothing more than a dull and dreary copy of the story itself. Instead, we will focus on the archetypal and cultural aspects, as these are less familiar to most readers. However, it is important to emphasise that both of these are also in service to an understanding of the characters as individuals. Only when we understand the heroes against the social and cultural world to which they belong can we truly appreciate their agency and individuality.

We have sketched some of the cultural background to Much Ado About Nothing, let's now turn to the archetypal perspective. Remember that the archetypes entail the four categories of identity, the biological-familial, the economic, the political (including military), and the religious. Love stories in Shakespeare always end in marriage, and we know that marriage is the consummation of a mature Adult identity in the biological-familial domain. Characters who are not married have not attained this aspect of Adult identity and they are therefore Orphans, at least in respect of their biological-familial identity. That can be true even though the individual is an Adult in the other domains of identity. This is the case for Benedick, who is a seasoned campaigner in battle and therefore has a mature economic and political identity. We would say he is an Adult in this respect and an Orphan in relation to his familial identity. Claudio is in the same boat since he has just solidified his Adult economic and political identity by proving himself in the recent battle.

For the women in the story, the situation is very different. In order to see why, we need to delve a little into the differences between the sexes that held in Shakespeare's time. Recall that the Orphan phase of life is the beginning of our identity in the economic, political, and religious domains. The onset of puberty ushers in the start of the Orphan archetype. In the biological-familial domain, this marks the time of sexual maturity and opens the possibility for marriage. In most cultures throughout history, marriage occurs quite soon after puberty for women, but not necessarily for men. Therein lies a crucial gender asymmetry that cuts across all the domains of identity.

For the aristocracy of Renaissance Italy, the setting in which Much Ado About Nothing takes place, the primary identity for Adult men was military in nature. Political identity was directly tied to this. An aristocratic man needed to be proficient in war. This was true of the lower-level aristocracy and even of kings. Meanwhile, the economic identity of the aristocracy was tied to ownership of landed estates and the agricultural wealth they created. That is how it had been since ancient times. The beginnings of what would later be called capitalism were only just sprouting in the Renaissance.

For aristocratic women of the same era, things were very different. There was certainly no military identity available to them, and their political and economic identity was subordinate to that of their husbands. Women were also denied access to mainstream religious roles and the educational system that corresponded to them. Nunneries were a fringe identity reserved mostly for women who had fallen out of normal society.

We can see that Claudio, Benedick, Don Pedro, and Leonato all fit the bill for the default aristocratic masculine identity of their time. They are both accomplished soldiers and wealthy land owners. Meanwhile, Hero represents the typical young aristocratic lady. She is under the guardianship of her father, who will eventually give her away to a husband. Implied in this is that the household was the place for women. A woman transitioned from the household of her parents to that of her husband's family. Within our classification, we would therefore say that aristocratic women's identity was found within the biological-familial domain. That was true in the Orphan phase of life and the Adult. The political and economic identity of women was always subordinate to their father and husband. The Orphan-to-Adult transition for an aristocratic woman relinquished her status in the household of her father in favour of a new role in the household of her husband. That is why we can say that Claudio's proposed marriage to Hero would accomplish Hero's transition out of Orphan status and into Adult. It would also fulfil the last remaining element of Claudio's full Adult identity. It therefore represents the standard Orphan-to-Adult transformation for both of them. That is another reason why their story is a cliché.

At the start of the story, Hero is in the standard archetypal role of daughter. Beatrice is not. The first thing that is unusual is that she is not living in the household of her parents but in that of her uncle. She has escaped the confines of the family home and the expectation of marriage that comes with it. Beatrice has created a sphere of independence for herself which was highly unusual for a woman of her social class. All of this fits in with the unconventional nature of the Benedick-Beatrice story as it would have appeared to Elizabethan audiences.

What's particularly interesting about this is that Beatrice's separation from her parents is exactly what makes her an Orphan. In fact, if we think about it more closely, we can see that the aristocratic women of this era almost did not have an Orphan phase of life. They went from being Children under the protection of the father straight to being married to their husbands. They went directly from the Child to the Adult. From an archetypal point of view, what makes Beatrice unique is that she is a female Orphan at a time when such a role barely existed in the general culture. The character of Beatrice is highly prophetic because the world in which we now live affords women an equally lengthy Orphan phase of life as men. That is why the love story between Beatrice and Benedick resonates so strongly with modern audiences.

Beatrice is the odd one out because it was expected that aristocratic men in the Renaissance era would establish themselves in society before looking to marry. Benedick may be in his late twenties or early thirties, but it was not uncommon for a man to marry at that age. Where Benedick is unusual is that he claims he does not want to marry. Still, it is Beatrice who is the most unique of the four heroes of the story.

Summing up, from the archetypal point of view, we would say that the story begins with four heroes who are all Orphans from the point of love and marriage. Hero and Claudio are going to follow the standard script that had been told in countless Renaissance love stories. They fall in love at first sight and become engaged. Benedick and Beatrice have, to use a modern term, a lot more *baggage* to work through because they have a history of failed romance with each other and have subsequently built their identity around the pain that came from that. It is their love story that was unique in Shakespeare's time.

But Shakespeare's innovations do not end there. From an archetypal point of view, he provides us with a unique Father figure in Leonato and, even more interestingly, an Elder character in Don Pedro.

Let's talk first about Leonato, who is the sole parent in the story. Leonato is the biological father of Hero and the legal father (guardian) of Beatrice. Shakespeare raises the stakes for Leonato by making Hero his sole heir, meaning that his estate will pass down to her and the man she will marry. This means Leonato's legacy rests on the successful marriage of his daughter. The responsibility is on him alone. This raises a very common theme that appears in many of Shakespeare's works where a father fumbles the difficult transition of power and wealth to the next generation. King Lear is the most dramatic and complex example, but we see the same dynamic with Leonato. It is worth briefly touching on why there are so many single fathers in Shakespeare's works.

Among the aristocracy in Shakespeare's time, marriage was almost entirely an economic and political transaction. The feelings of the married couple toward each other were irrelevant. Esoteric love was not required. Marriages were organised by parents according to political and economic calculation. That is why the action in Much Ado About Nothing is unusual from the very beginning because the couples are coming together through love, not through duty and obligation.

In accordance with the pragmatic view of marriage that dominated in this era, especially among the aristocracy, a young wife's primary role was to give birth to heirs. Because infant mortality was high, and because the wealthy had the resources to afford it, large families were desirable. However, childbirth was dangerous, and the threat to the mother was additive over time. Possibly as high as ten per cent of aristocratic women died in childbirth while fulfilling their obligations to propagate the family line. That's one reason why single fathers existed.

The second and more important reason why aristocratic mothers would be absent at the time their children reached marriageable age was because, once the duty of childbearing was fulfilled, husbands and wives often chose to live separately. This was common among the aristocracy who could afford the expense of maintaining separate households. Because of the patriarchal basis of the laws at this time, the father was the legal guardian, and the children would live with him. As high as one third of aristocratic marriages followed this pattern of physical separation, meaning that the situation shown in stories such as King Lear and Much Ado About Nothing really was quite common at the time Shakespeare was writing. It was the father who had the legal and moral obligation to oversee the marriage of his children. If mothers were present, they could have an important informal role, as we see in Romeo and Juliet, but ultimate authority rested with the father.

This cultural background reveals something about the character of Leonato that is not obvious to us in modern times. He does not take a business-like attitude to the marriage of Hero. In fact, we can see from the opening scenes of the villa and his involvement in the details of the masquerade ball that Leonato is a man of culture and refinement who clearly takes pleasure in the finer things in life. His encouragement of the love affairs of both Hero and Beatrice is testament to this. These qualities endear him to modern audiences. However, Elizabethan audiences may very well have seen him as reckless for risking the marriage of his only daughter. This is especially true because Leonato's attitude is somewhat responsible for the sacred part of the story where everything goes wrong. In fact, Leonato's own identity crisis results from his encouragement of esoteric love. This is true of all of the characters, but it was highly unusual in the Father character of a Renaissance love story. Thus, Leonato is arguably as unique a character as his niece Beatrice.

The fourth unique character is Don Pedro. He is the mentor to Claudio and has just initiated the younger man into the world of military action. That was all perfectly normal for the time and would have earned Don Pedro the everlasting gratitude of Claudio and his family. What was not normal was that a man like Don Pedro would become a matchmaker, guiding the Orphans of the story through their transformation towards marriage. This follows logically from the fact that aristocratic marriage was normally organised by parents for political and economic reasons. But we can also see why Don Pedro is unique by comparing against the standard pattern of the classical love story.

In ancient Greece and Rome, the esoteric love of the two heroes in a romance is initiated by the gods. Perhaps the most famous example of this is the role played by Aphrodite in making Helen fall in love with Paris, which leads to the Trojan War. Where a human matchmaker appeared in a classical narrative, the story was invariably a comedy, and what was at stake was not love but sex. The matchmakers in these stories practised deception in order to bring the couple together. The comedic aspect was heightened by the fact that the couple were not really in love but just wanted to have a fling, something that could only be done by going behind the backs of their families. Thus, the matchmaker would spend most of the story trying to deceive the family members so that they did not discover the young couple's dalliance.

As he so often does, Shakespeare takes these familiar tropes and adapts them to his own purposes. Don Pedro ends up playing something like the role of matchmaker from the classical comedy, since he uses deception to bring the couples together. However, he is also playing the role of the gods because his efforts are intended to engender love, not merely sex. In fact, Shakespeare has Don Pedro tell us explicitly that he is taking over from the gods. Of his cunning plan to bring Benedick and Beatrice together, he tells the others, "If we can do this, Cupid is no longer an archer; his glory shall be ours, for we are the only love-gods."

Another twist is that Don Pedro does not deceive the other characters in the story, as was common for the matchmaker in classical comedies. Instead, he deceives the lovers themselves. His deception of Benedick and Beatrice is intended to make them admit their own feelings. The two cynics who have built up intellectual defences against love will be ushered into the sacred by being made to believe that the other already loves them. Meanwhile, Don

Pedro also practises a form of deception at the beginning of the story by wooing Hero on Claudio's behalf.

This larger cultural transition away from the gods and towards a strictly human love saw an intermediate stage in Chaucer's "Troilus and Criseyde" where the hero is made to fall in love by a god but where the love story relies on a human intermediary, Pandarus. By the time of Shakespeare, the gods had been removed altogether, and their role falls explicitly to Don Pedro. Because Don Pedro is merely giving the heroes what they want anyway, the responsibility does not fall solely on him but the lovers too. That is the price to be paid when humans take over. The gods are no longer around to be blamed when things go wrong. All of this is perfectly in keeping with Shakespeare's *oeuvre* in general. All of the Bard's heroes are held responsible for their errors and vices. That is why their journey through the sacred is always first and foremost one of self-discovery.

To recap, the classical love story, whether in tragic or comic form, involved a clash between the lovers and their families which pitted esoteric love against exoteric notions of duty and honour. This conflict was facilitated by either the gods or a human matchmaker. Shakespeare famously uses the theme of familial strife in the love story of Romeo and Juliet. However, in Much Ado About Nothing, Don Pedro and Leonato happen to be great friends. As a result, there is no friction at all between the lovers and their family. On the contrary, Leonato encourages the esoteric love between them. Without this friction, there should be nothing to stop their love from being easily consummated in marriage. That is true of the relationship between Hero and Claudio, which looks certain to end happily. Enter Shakespeare's final innovation. The source of conflict will come from another human character who is the inversion of the matchmaker and also his brother: the miserable Don John.

If Don Pedro is the Elder guiding the Orphans of the story towards love and marriage, Don John functions as his shadow, the anti-Elder. He does so by engaging the same tactic that Don Pedro uses: deception. Moreover, it is Don John who triggers the troubles that play a core component in the classical love story: the man's pride and the woman's honour. Since a woman's chastity determined her entire ability to be married in the first place, if she was found to have violated it, that was a life-changing event that often ended with enrolment in a nunnery. That is why esoteric love conducted outside the bounds of formal relationships was seen to be so dangerous. It was also very common for a threat to the woman's honour to be met with violence on the part of her family, either towards her or towards her lover. Either way, love could go very wrong when honour entered the equation.

It is no surprise, then, that Don John's devious scheme involves bringing Hero's honour into question and, in doing so, to challenge the pride of Claudio, Don Pedro, and Leonato. In the classical love story, these questions of honour and shame arose by default whenever esoteric love took place precisely because marriage was an exoteric arrangement where love was entirely optional. A love that arose esoterically was always a risk and, therefore, sacred. Because Leonato encourages the esoteric love between Claudio and Hero, Shakespeare needs another way to bring the primary risk into the story, and he does so by way of Don John. What would normally be left up to the gods or "nature" now has a human instigator. Just as Don Pedro is trying to win for himself the power previously reserved for deities, so too is Don John exercising a new kind of role, the curmudgeon who wants to destroy love just because. In any case, the descent into the sacred that occurs in Much Ado About Nothing does follow the classical pattern of bringing the woman's chastity into question and thereby threatening the honour of herself and her family. The major difference is that these problems no longer arise automatically but have a human source, and if they have a human source, they also have a human solution.

Because the concept of honour has almost entirely disappeared from modern Western culture, we need to take the time to understand it better. Fortunately, we already have exactly the concept we need: the difference between the esoteric and exoteric poles of existence.

Honour refers to the way in which we are perceived by our society. To have honour is to be well-regarded. To be dishonourable is to be poorly-regarded due to bad behaviour. Honour is exoteric. Pride is the esoteric feeling that corresponds to honour. If I win a sporting competition, honour is the external reward I get while pride is the inner feeling I experience. Where honour is deserved, pride is not a bad thing, and the exoteric and esoteric are in equilibrium. However, the two can get out of sync. It is possible to be honoured for things that one does not feel pride in. Similarly, it is possible to feel pride in achievements that win us no honour. In these cases, the esoteric and exoteric are out of balance. A core part of the journey into the sacred comes from this imbalance between the esoteric and exoteric aspects of our identity and the need to rediscover equilibrium.

The balance between Hero's exoteric and esoteric identities is thrown out when Don John successfully deceives Don Pedro and Claudio into thinking she is seeing another man on the side. When they accuse her in public, her honour is shattered. Since she did not actually commit the deed, she cannot feel the esoteric emotions of shame or conscience that may lead to atonement. Her exoteric identity is threatened by something she has no esoteric connection with. Where our exoteric and esoteric identities diverge from each other, we are un-whole, unholy, and unhealthy. Hero is both publicly tarnished and psychologically distraught at the unjust accusations levelled against her. Leonato undergoes a similar crisis in that the honour of his family has been attacked and his chances of handing over his legacy to the next generation ruined.

In the classical love story, all of this happened automatically as an act of the gods or nature. But Shakespeare has introduced Don John to be the very human cause of the threat to Hero's honour. We might be tempted, therefore, to lay the blame entirely at his feet. But, in truth, all of the characters have brought it on themselves because they willingly undertook the journey into the sacred. Don Pedro made the choice to attempt to win the power of the gods by becoming a matchmaker. He had willing accomplices in Claudio, Leonato, and even Hero, all of whom join in the deception of Benedick and Beatrice. They are all, to use the famous phrase from Hamlet, hoisted by their own petard, the weapon of deception turned back on themselves. This is a recurring theme in all of Shakespeare's greatest works, and it follows from the fact that Shakespeare's heroes willingly pursue their own transformation.

We must remember that the identity crisis that the hero faces is not a purely reactionary event. The hero must be prepared to sacrifice their existing identity. But, at the exact same time, the hero is working towards something new. This sets up an almost mathematical equation. The sacrifice must be proportional to the reward. Claudio wants Hero for his wife, but rather than do the work himself, he allows Don Pedro to woo her on his behalf. He attempts to get something for nothing. Don Pedro wants to accrue to himself the power of matchmaker, but he must learn that this comes with its own set of risks. Leonato wants to encourage esoteric love, but perhaps there was some wisdom in the traditional beliefs that saw this as a danger rather than an unmitigated blessing. He must learn the hard way.

Alongside pride and honour, this introduces a third concept: hubris. Hubris is the reckless striving after an identity we do not have a right to. The classical meaning of hubris was presumption towards the gods. Don Pedro is literally guilty of that by presuming to acquire the power of Cupid. The other characters who join with him share the responsibility. Arguably, Beatrice and Benedick are guilty of hubris for pretending that they are unique when it comes to love and marriage and that the "rules" do not apply to them.

In the classical world, hubris brought ruin. The characters in Much Ado About Nothing would have been seen by classical and Renaissance audiences to invite the same fate, but Shakespeare suggests something very different by giving the story a happy ending, and this leads to one of the major cultural shifts that his work ushered in to Western culture.

On what grounds can we say somebody does not have a right to a new identity that they are striving for? Where is the objective criteria to declare somebody reckless and presumptuous? How may we know that somebody is guilty of hubris? In truth, there are no objective criteria when it comes to such matters. They belong in the inherent grey area of the sacred where holy concepts such as objective truth do not apply. What Shakespeare implies is that it is not a question of presumption or morality but of sacrifice. We may wish for anything we like, but we must pay the price for it.

Does this mean that hubris doesn't exist? Arguably, we will see hubris in perhaps its most extreme form when we come to examine Macbeth. It is also central to the story in Julius Caesar. It is the belief that Caesar has fallen into hubris that motivates Brutus to help with his assassination. Nevertheless,

Shakespeare makes it ambiguous whether Caesar really has crossed the line, since it's not clear whether he really wants to become ruler. But, even if he did, on what grounds do we call that illegitimate hubris rather than legitimate ambition? At the very least, Shakespeare places a very large question mark over the whole notion of hubris.

The journey into the sacred is the confrontation with the fundamental ambiguities in life. What one person calls ambition, another calls hubris. We can't know in advance where the line is or when we will cross it. Macbeth was ambitious and got rewarded for his virtuous actions. That tempted him into hubris. While Macbeth is clearly in the wrong for killing Duncan and stealing his throne, we would say that Hamlet was in the wrong for not killing Claudius and taking his rightful place on the throne. Macbeth is hubristic. Hamlet is overly casual and blasé. But all of this is only known after the fact. Only in the holy state at the end of the story may we make such judgements. While the story is underway, there is always the chance that the hero finds the balance and reconnects with a holy identity in the end.

We can see then that the issues of pride and honour that form the basis of the drama in Much Ado About Nothing are more generally applicable to every story because every story requires the hero to transform themselves. Every hero is required to renegotiate the interface between pride and honour as their esoteric understanding of their identity and the exoteric one that comes from society come into conflict. Only when these have been brought into alignment can the hero return to holy state.

What Shakespeare intimates, at least in relation to love, is that pride is often just a cover for fear. If we wish to create for ourselves a new identity, then we must be prepared to take a hit to our honour. That is true by definition because honour is our exoteric identity and it is that identity that we must relinquish. Claudio tries to avoid this risk by having Don Pedro act on his behalf. He is not willing to risk the damage to his honour that would come from a rejection by Hero. He fears the loss of his exoteric identity. Leonato's pride is also motivated by a fear of loss. Because Hero is his sole heir, Leonato's estate and his bloodline are at stake. When confronted with an unexpected sacrifice of his honour, he responds by projecting his fear onto his daughter. In doing so, he leaves her in the lurch. Benedick's and Beatrice's pride is tied to the loss of the identity that both have constructed, whereby they claim to have sworn off marriage and love altogether.

In the end, the sacrifice they all must make is to accept a major challenge to their honour, one that threatens to become permanent. As Benedick explains to us during one of his soliloquies in the story, love makes one a fool. A lover must always be prepared to look foolish for love. That is fitting in a love story where no great matters of economics, politics, or religion are at stake. We may be tempted to write it off as a minor idea in the greater pantheon of Shakespeare's work. There are two things to say about that.

Firstly, the hero of every story must risk their honour because honour is always tied to the identity that the hero has in the beginning. Honour is nothing more or less than the exoteric identity of the hero that is recognised and understood by their family, friends, and wider society. Since every transformation requires a change of identity, it follows that the honour of the hero is always at risk. Sacrificing honour is a necessary part of the journey into the sacred. The challenge is to come out the other side with one's honour tied to a new identity.

Secondly, on the question of love, the "foolishness" of sacrificing honour for love implies a value judgement that love is not worth the trouble. To sacrifice honour for material gain and political power - that was understood by the ancients. To sacrifice it for love made one a fool, not in the romantic sense but in the intellectual one, as in, you'd have to be dumb to even try it. Benedick also meditates on this during his soliloquy. Claudio has seemingly turned away from the mentality of a soldier to pursue that of a lover. He is now concerned with the finer things in life like music, clothing, and dancing. Benedick asks the question: are these trivial matters set apart from the real business of life, or are they the most important part of life? The classical world assumed the former was true. Shakespeare intimates the latter.

Compared to the "real world" of military battle, love seems ephemeral and illusory. That is why both Don Pedro and Don John must use deception. Doesn't that make it unreal, false, and fictitious? But Don Pedro "deceives" Benedick and Beatrice only by making them admit what was already in their hearts: their love for each other. Perhaps love reveals the deepest truths of all, and perhaps we become most truthful when we are most foolish.

Romeo and Juliet

Our use of the archetypes as a representation of developmental phases makes the question of time explicit in our analysis in the sense that we locate the hero at a specific point in their life. This is not an ideological or theoretical viewpoint. It is common sense. However, by making it explicit, we are able to draw out implications that normally go unnoticed. Shakespeare's stories almost always feature a hero that is at an archetypal turning point in their lives. King Lear has reached old age. Hamlet has reached maturity. Othello has just got married. These are major changes on life's journey. The hero must transition out of one phase of life and into a qualitatively different one. The transitions between the archetypes make natural stories, transformations that we all must go through.

Why does Claudio fall in love with Hero at just the time he does? Is it pure chance that comes only from the fact that his mentor, Don Pedro, decides to stop by and visit Leonato? That is certainly one aspect of it. But the other side of the coin is that Claudio is ready to marry. The time is right. We know from Benedick's teasing that, only months earlier, the only thing Claudio cared about was glory in battle. But now he is returning from battle having proven himself. The political and economic aspects of his Adult identity are fulfilled. He is ready to marry. Although meant sardonically, Jane Austen's famous opening line is relevant here: "It is a truth universally acknowledged that a single man in possession of a good fortune must be in want of a wife."

We may think of the archetypes as structures that contain spaces that need to be filled. When we move to a new archetype, we need to fill the spaces. But we must also relinquish those of the old archetype we are transitioning away from. The "spaces" have an exoteric and an esoteric pole. Both of these must be satisfied, but the process never happens synchronously. This is another way in which time comes into the equation because an imbalance between the esoteric and exoteric takes time to get back to equilibrium. Claudio is esoterically in love. His challenge becomes how to exoterically consummate it. The esoteric precedes the exoteric in this case. However, it can happen the other way around too. Benedick and Beatrice receive some gentle teasing from the other characters in the story about their unmarried status. It is the exoteric realm that is prompting them to discover an esoteric aspect of their identity.

This back and forth between the exoteric and esoteric forms a kind of rhythm that sits beneath the surface of Shakespeare's stories. An esoteric space becomes vacant; it must be fulfilled exoterically. An exoteric component of identity is holding the hero back; it must be relinquished. Claudio's esoteric love leads to an exoteric marriage proposal. He falls back into the esoteric with the deception of Don John, makes an exoteric accusation that derails everything, and finally must exoterically atone for his error. The beats of a story form a rhythm. Sometimes, it is forceful and inevitable, as in Macbeth. Sometimes, it is halting and intricate, as in Hamlet. Sometimes, it rushes forward like a dam bursting, as in King Lear.

Much Ado About Nothing is a comedy, and that means the heroes successfully navigate the transformation of their identity, bringing the esoteric and exoteric into alignment by the end of the story and consecrating their completed Adult identities. In Shakespeare's tragedies, this does not happen. The identity crisis becomes a wound that does not heal. That is absolutely the case in his most famous love story, Romeo and Juliet.

Since this play is probably Shakespeare's most famous, with perhaps only the exception of Hamlet, we need pay little to no attention to the main body of the story, including the initial meeting at the ball and the classic balcony scene. Instead, we will focus on those parts of the story that are not so well-remembered or understood in our time and which made the story unique in Shakespeare's. We have already outlined why Much Ado About Nothing was special by comparing it against the typical Renaissance love story. Nominally,

Romeo and Juliet is an example of the cliché of that era: the love-at-first-sight story. But it wouldn't be the greatest love story of all time if it were nothing more than a cliché. As he always did, Shakespeare found ways to utilise the standard components in a way that created something new and fresh. Fortunately, we already have the perfect starting point to begin our analysis because Romeo and Juliet are in almost the same archetypal situation as Claudio and Hero, albeit with a number of minor differences that nevertheless add up to something more profound.

Recall that Claudio begins his story having just accomplished a major milestone of proving his valour in battle. That means he has taken a firm step into a mature Adult economic and political identity, which in turn leads to him looking for a wife. It's no coincidence that Claudio has a strong mentor in Don Pedro to guide him through the final stages of what would be his Orphan phase of life. By the end of the story, Claudio has become an Adult in all categories of our identity model.

Compare Claudio against the group we meet at the beginning of Romeo and Juliet. The young men of Verona are not off fighting glorious battles in foreign lands. They are fighting each other on the streets of their home town and causing their neighbours and families a great deal of trouble in the process. We learn from the opening scene that this has been the norm for some time. Prince Escalus' announcement of the death penalty for any further violence shows that the issue is now coming to a head in the exoteric realm. But the threat of punishment does not address the underlying problem, which is that the young men are stuck in the Orphan phase of life. Unlike Claudio, they are not moving towards a mature, Adult identity. In fact, they are flirting with the destruction of their identity altogether if Prince Escalus follows through with his threat.

Romeo is part of this group, and we presume that he has also dabbled in a bit of street fighting. However, he is not present for the opening kerfuffle because he is off pining for a young woman, Rosaline, who will not reciprocate his affections. The implication here is that Romeo has done exactly what Claudio does in the opening scene of Much Ado, namely, fallen in love at first sight. The key difference is that Romeo is in no position to marry even if Rosaline were interested. He is striving after a familial identity that is denied to him just as the other young men are lacking an economic and military identity that would lead them to something more productive than brawling.

It follows from this that Romeo, his friends, and the whole city of Verona are in sacred state when the story begins. That means we must spend the time to identify Romeo's holy state using the clues laid out by Shakespeare with his technique of covert exposition. The key detail in this respect is the scene after the fighting where we see Romeo's parents asking his cousin where he is. Benvolio tells them that he is sulking away somewhere as usual, and they express worry at the fact that he has become a recluse. Two points follow from this. Firstly, it is implied that Romeo has only recently had this problem, meaning he must have fallen in love with Rosaline in just the last few weeks. Secondly, the fact that he has become partially estranged from his parents indicates that he is in the Orphan archetypal phase. That is also true of the fighting that is going on more broadly. What we have in Verona is a group of young men whose parents cannot control them. They are in the Orphan phase of life, but there is no Don Pedro around to keep them away from trouble.

The absence of a wise mentor is also a more direct reason for Romeo's troubles. The girl he has fallen for is a Capulet, and the street fight that begins the story informs us that the Montagues and Capulets are at war with each other. Therefore, apart from all the other problems that Romeo has got, he has fallen for a girl that he could never marry in the first place. Contrast this with the dynamic in Much Ado, where Don Pedro is close friends with Leonato and therefore Claudio's marriage to Hero is all but guaranteed. Romeo has no matchmaker who can help him towards a love that can actually have a chance at succeeding.

Thus, Romeo has entered the Orphan phase of life with nobody to guide him. He and his friends have no meaningful identities to pursue, and so they are dabbling in crime with the force of the law now hanging over them. Romeo is in an even worse situation than the others because he has fallen head over heels in love with a woman who does not like him and with whom he has no prospects anyway. Romeo is languishing. That is the sacred state we find him in when the action begins, and we can presume that, prior to all this, he was a well-adjusted young boy with parents who cared for him and no real troubles in the world.

All of this is already a departure from the standard love-at-first-sight story from the Renaissance. Things veer even more off the beaten track when Juliet is introduced, and, once again, it is the role of the parent where Shakespeare innovated in ways that the modern reader is unlikely to perceive.

Unlike Romeo, Juliet begins the story in holy state, and we see directly the event which precipitates her identity crisis and transition into sacred state. To grasp this, we must remember the gender asymmetry we discussed in Much Ado About Nothing. Juliet is a young lady of the aristocracy who, until now, has been safely tucked away in her family home with the nurse that has raised her still by her side. At thirteen years old, she was considered old enough to marry by the society of her time, a fact that is reinforced when Juliet's own mother reminds her that not only had her friends already married but some of them were already mothers. Therefore, there is nothing unusual in the fact that Paris pays a visit to Lord Capulet to ask for Juliet's hand in marriage. What is highly unusual is Lord Capulet's response:-

> Paris: "But now, my lord, what do you say to my suit?"
>
> Capulet: "By saying o'er what I have said before. My child is yet a stranger in the world".

Capulet thinks that Juliet is still too young even though such a marriage was not at all out of the ordinary for a young aristocratic lady of her time. This tells us something very important about Capulet. Paris is not just any suitor. He is probably the most eligible suitor in the whole of Verona since he belongs to the family of the ruler, Prince Escalus. When we remember that aristocratic marriages in the Renaissance were conducted entirely for economic and political purposes, we can see that Capulet's reluctance marks him as the kind of man who is not just in it for the money. He genuinely cares about his daughter and wants her to be happy. In this way, Capulet is very similar to Leonato in Much Ado. Both are men of refinement and culture who are not primarily interested in wealth and political power.

Shakespeare reinforces this by having Capulet actively encourage love between Paris and Juliet. After initially refusing the young man's proposal, he tells him he will assent to the marriage on the condition that Juliet falls in love:-

> But woo her, gentle Paris, get her heart
> My will to her consent is but a part,
> And, she agree, within her scope of choice
> Lies my consent and fair according voice

To those of us in the modern West, there is nothing at all to disagree with in this passage. Of course Juliet should choose who she marries. Of course she should marry a man that she is in love with. Nevertheless, we must reiterate that this idea of marrying for love was radical for its time, even more so because it does not come from Juliet herself but from her father. Paris has come to Capulet with a very business-like proposal that was perfectly in keeping with aristocratic marriage customs. Capulet rejects it and replaces it with something different. He organises a ball and invites the whole town. He puts on delicious food, delightful music, and all the other accoutrements of refinement, and then he invites Paris with the express instruction for him to make Juliet fall in love. None of this is necessary in a practical sense. None of it is expected by the culture of the time. It doesn't make financial or political sense. Capulet is going out of his way to create the conditions for love.

As if that wasn't enough, Lady Capulet gets in on the action too. Immediately afterwards, she pays a visit to her daughter in her bedroom. She asks whether Juliet has ever thought of marriage. Juliet replies, "It is an honour I dreamt not of". Remember, the concept of honour refers explicitly to exoteric identity. Juliet thinks of marriage in this formal, structural sense. It is a duty to be performed. Thus, both Paris and Juliet, the younger people in this dynamic, think of marriage as entirely a political and business proposition.

Lady Capulet then sets out to change that. After remarking on her daughter's use of the word "honour", she asks a more specific and direct question:

"Can you love the gentleman?" Juliet says she doesn't know. Her mother instructs her to attend the ball that evening and gives her a guide on what to look for in Paris. Juliet's own mother is trying to encourage esoteric love in her daughter, who has clearly never thought about it before.

To understand what is really going on in this scenario, we must recall our distinction between the exoteric and esoteric poles of existence. We noted earlier that the Child phase of life is marked by the absence of exoteric identity. The Child's identity is subsumed entirely within the family. Meanwhile, the esoteric dimensions of childhood are well known and include the wonder of imagination and play, the freedom from responsibility, etc. The transition from Child to Orphan is difficult precisely because these attributes must be given up. In the exoteric domain, the individual must begin their integration into the broader society by joining the institutions that bestow on them economic, political, and religious rights and responsibilities. This is normally done with the aid of an Elder character who guides and educates the Orphan. The problem that Romeo and his friends have is that they have not received this initiation and they have no wise mentor to guide them.

On the esoteric side of the ledger, the challenges of the Orphan transition are also well known. Puberty brings with it the emotional rollercoaster of hormonal changes. There is the discovery of sexual desire. There is a sudden interest in meaning and purpose that comes with the onset of the age of reason. There is a strong desire to fit in and find one's place in a social grouping and an equally strong fear of being left out. That's why it is inappropriate for a young person to show no desire to socialise since the goal of the Orphan phase of life is to establish an identity in society. Thus, Romeo's reclusion is a genuine problem, and his parents are right to be worried.

In the case of love and marriage, the former is the esoteric component and the latter the exoteric. When we say that aristocratic marriage was concerned entirely with political and economic calculations, that is another way of saying that it was entirely unconcerned with love and other esoteric dimensions. That is why the behaviour of Lord and Lady Capulet is so unusual.

Returning now to Juliet, what Shakespeare effortlessly and concisely establishes with the scenes we have just mentioned is that she has been securely in the Child phase of life up until now. Her statement to her mother that she has not thought about marriage and has no idea what it means to find a man attractive tells us that she has not taken the esoteric step into the Orphan phase of life. She thinks of marriage entirely in its exoteric form of "honour". She doesn't know about esoteric love. That is why her mother needs to tell her about it.

Thus, the identity crisis that faces Juliet has its origin in the exoteric realm. Paris has not tried to woo her, meaning he has also not thought about esoteric love. Rather, he is taking the formal, exoteric approach that was perfectly in keeping with the marriage customs of the Renaissance aristocracy. What any normal pair of aristocratic parents would have done was to thank their lucky stars that their daughter had been chosen by such a well-connected young man. They would have arranged the marriage as soon as possible so he wouldn't have the time to change his mind. But Lord and Lady Capulet are not concerned with that. They are concerned with the esoteric. Thus, it is Juliet's own parents who are trying to translate an exoteric marriage proposal into esoteric love. They are encouraging her esoteric progression into the Orphan phase of life. That is the identity crisis that sees Juliet take the leap into the sacred.

Shakespeare takes the same unusual dynamic that we saw in Much Ado About Nothing and amplifies it in Romeo and Juliet. In the former story, Leonato takes an active approach to encouraging the love of Benedick and Beatrice but only a passive one in relation to his daughter, Hero. It is Don Pedro who is the instigator of that relationship. In Romeo and Juliet, we have Lord and Lady Capulet themselves trying to spark the esoteric transition of Juliet from Child to Orphan, thereby opening the way to exoteric marriage. This was deeply unusual for aristocratic weddings where, mostly, the bride and groom would never even meet before the wedding day, so there could be no question of esoteric love or attraction. If love did happen to follow marriage, that was all well and good, but it was not considered important. The most important thing was the propagation of the family line, including the wealth and social status of the family.

It is clear that Shakespeare was perfectly well aware of all this because he has Laertes give the following lecture to his sister, Ophelia, on her relationship with Prince Hamlet:-

Perhaps he loves you now,
And now no soil nor cautel doth besmirch
The virtue of his will: but you must fear
His greatness weigh'd, his will is not his own;
For he himself is subject to his birth:
He may not, as unvalued persons do,
Carve for himself; for, on his choice depends
The sanctity and health of the whole State,
And therefore must his choice be circumscrib'd
Unto the voice and yielding of that body,
Whereof he is the head

Laertes is informing Ophelia that, even if Hamlet really loves her, his choice of bride is not his own but will be dictated by the national interest of Denmark. Since she is not in contention for an exoteric union, the only result of their esoteric dalliance will be the loss of her honour. This exoteric approach to marriage remained mostly true for European aristocracy and royalty well into the 19th century, and it had been practised ever since ancient times.

When viewed against this cultural and political background, we can see that Romeo and Juliet is actually the harbinger of a change that had just started to take place in Britain during the Elizabethan era. Aristocratic parents began to at least consider the opinions of their children when arranging marriages. The idea that marriage should include esoteric love alongside exoteric duty also slowly became acceptable. Since duty to one's parents was still expected, it is somewhat fitting that Lord and Lady Capulet take the lead in encouraging Paris and Juliet to develop an esoteric attraction before committing to an exoteric union.

Although they have very different pathways into the transformation, what we see is that the identity crisis that faces both Romeo and Juliet is esoteric in nature. In Romeo's case, this has happened "naturally" since young men do not normally need any extra encouragement to develop attraction to the opposite sex. Juliet's example is more unusual because her own parents are prompting her to look at men for the first time. Their hope is that she will fall in love with Paris and then a marriage can follow shortly thereafter. That is what is supposed to take place at the ball which Lord Capulet has arranged. Romeo has snuck in, hoping to find Rosaline. Juliet is there with instructions from her mother to pay attention to Paris. Instead, they find each other.

All of this represents a major innovation of the classic love-at-first-sight story that had been around since medieval times. But Shakespeare is not just innovating for the sake of it. Something very important is being expressed by the changes he makes.

One of the main tropes of the classic version of the story was that the lovers were "made for each other". What this means is that some kind of higher power brought them together, whether it be God, or the stars, or something like that. Shakespeare goes out of his way to make clear that it is not a matter of Romeo and Juliet being "made for each other" or that they are brought together by "fate" or the gods or what have you. Their first meeting, which takes place at the Capulet ball, has two sources. Romeo is there by his own daring, since he is sneaking into a place where he is likely to be killed in order to catch a glimpse of Rosaline. Juliet is there by the order of her parents, who are hoping she will fall in love with Paris and who have primed her for that exact eventuality. None of this is accidental. Romeo is looking for love. The Capulets are hoping their daughter will find it. Everything has been set up to create esoteric love. It is not a matter of fate where the princess is wandering by a stream and the handsome prince stumbles across her. It has been done on purpose.

This wilful and deliberate aspect to the broader context is then shown by Romeo and Juliet themselves because, while they are there for other reasons, what occurs is that they choose each other. They are not brought together by fate or by some mystical union. They fall in love because the conditions have been created to allow esoteric love to occur and because both of them choose to pursue it. Romeo has chosen because he has broken in the Capulet's ball for that purpose. Juliet has chosen because she is not following her parents' advice. The fact that both of them were supposed to be looking for somebody else serves to heighten their free choice in each other. Shakespeare is not subverting the idea that you can fall in love at first sight; he is negating the notion that it happens for some higher purpose.

Having established that Romeo and Juliet are making their own choice, Shakespeare then instantly raises the stakes by having them realise that the choice is one that is forbidden to them because they are Montague and Capulet. If they want to pursue their love, they will need to make a sacrifice. Now the real identity crisis begins. Their exoteric identity comes into conflict with their esoteric one. Romeo can count on being put to death if he is found out. Juliet will destroy her honour and be banished from her family. The stakes are existential for both of them. That is why they must keep their love a secret in the first instance.

The result is a complete split between the esoteric and exoteric. More specifically, what Shakespeare ends up showing us in Romeo and Juliet is esoteric love in its purest form, entirely decoupled from any of the grimy exoteric considerations of aristocratic marriage. He shows us two lovers who are prepared to risk their own lives for their love. If the magnitude of a story may be judged by the sacrifice which the hero is prepared to make, then there can be no higher sacrifice than one's own life. By subverting the "made for each other" trope of the love-at-first-sight story, Shakespeare delivers us a brand new kind of love story, one in which the heroes take on the highest responsibility. Love is no longer left to the gods or to fate; it is pursued deliberately and consciously, and the risks involved are understood even by a young and inexperienced pair.

We can further tease out the new meanings that Shakespeare created by comparing them against the stories that he used as quarries for his ideas. We already know that Renaissance-era stories saw esoteric love as dangerous due to its threat to the chastity of the daughter and, by extension, the honour of the family. It was the duty of the father and brothers to uphold that honour, which they did with the pointy end of a sword. Thus, what we see in numerous love stories is that the man involved in the dalliance gets killed by the family of the woman when the illicit love is discovered. Shakespeare incorporates this theme into Romeo and Juliet. When Tybalt discovers Romeo at the Capulet ball, he wants to kill him. But, again, it is Lord Capulet who prevents violence and even shows a measure of sympathy for the young Montague. Such attitudes would never have been accepted two centuries earlier. The exoteric honour of the family and its daughter trumped all else. Once again, we find Juliet's parents taking a far more lenient approach and encouraging the esoteric over the exoteric.

Renaissance storytellers did not consider that option, and so they had two primary ways to avoid the tragic outcome and guide the story to a happy ending. The first was to have the lovers elope and thereby live happily ever after by getting married somewhere else. This successfully consummated the marriage but at the cost of their familial identities. The second type of happy ending was for some completely unexpected event to occur which allows a marriage to take place. This option was only valid where the esoteric dalliance could be kept secret so that the honour of the bride was maintained. Note that both of these outcomes bring the exoteric and esoteric into alignment.

Shakespeare brilliantly manages to incorporate both of these potential happy endings into his story. The first plan is for Romeo and Juliet to pull off a surprise marriage. The second plan is for them to elope. Either of these options would allow their exoteric and esoteric identities to be made whole again and their love to be consummated. What Shakespeare changes, however, is where responsibility lies. Once again, the crucial fact is that both of these options are deliberately pursued by Romeo and Juliet themselves. They do not fall backwards into an accidental marriage as was the case in the Renaissance story, and they do not elope out of a desire to escape from the immediate danger of violence. These ideas are deliberately and consciously enacted.

In fact, when we step back and view the story more broadly, we can see that Romeo and Juliet are the driving force behind events once they decide to pursue their love. Firstly, there is the fact that they agree to marry during the famous balcony scene. Secondly, Romeo immediately rushes off to Friar Lawrence to arrange the marriage. Thirdly, the marriage is actually carried out in a secret ceremony at the chapel. Viewed esoterically, all of this represents the successful consummation of love and marriage. But that is the whole problem: it has only taken place in the esoteric realm. Their family and wider society have no idea about it. Since these actions do not bring the esoteric and exoteric into alignment, they cannot achieve the holy state that is desired.

That is where Friar Lawrence comes into the picture, and it is fascinating that Shakespeare once again introduces an Elder character into a love story. It is Lawrence's plan to marry the young couple in secret and then make the marriage an exoteric fact by presenting it as a *fait accompli* to Romeo and Juliet's parents. All of this fits perfectly within our archetypal logic because we have two Orphan characters turning to an Elder for advice in the exact same way that Claudio turns to Don Pedro in Much Ado. But here we come across a crucial but incredibly subtle variation.

Unlike Don Pedro, who is motivated by a desire to win for himself the power of Cupid, Friar Lawrence is not interested in esoteric love. On the contrary, it is clear that he considers the behaviour of the young couple to be a little silly. His motivation for getting involved is that he believes he can use the marriage as a way to bring about a *rapprochement* between the Montagues and Capulets. What is crucial about this is that Lawrence is thinking about marriage exactly the way that was normal among the aristocracy of the time, i.e., in terms of social and political calculation. He is not a true believer in love like Don Pedro. Arguably, Lawrence is guilty of cynicism for thinking that he can use the young lovers for political purposes.

If so, his punishment comes almost instantly when the original plan fails due to Romeo's getting sucked into a fight and killing Tybalt. Prince Escalus shows leniency by sentencing him to banishment instead of death. This sets the scene for Plan B, which involves the young lovers eloping. Unable to establish a proper exoteric identity in their home town, they will need to create one elsewhere. As everybody knows, Lawrence's backup plan fails due to a communication breakdown leading to the famous final scene in the tomb. The result of all this is that the love of Romeo and Juliet remains entirely secret until it is too late. Only at the very end of the play does the esoteric truth become an exoteric fact, but by then they are already dead and there is nothing left for the parents to do but grieve. Romeo and Juliet do not complete their transformation. They fail to bring their esoteric and exoteric identities into balance.

What all the modifications that Shakespeare makes to the classical love story achieve is to make the characters responsible for their actions. That is true of Romeo and Juliet, who choose each other and then choose to be married even though they know the risks associated with it. It is true of Lord and Lady Capulet, who encourage their daughter to esoteric love. It is true of Romeo's parents, who allow him to go forth into society without any guidance at all. It is also true of Friar Lawrence, who does not really believe in love but takes a calculating approach to the whole affair. All of this follows from the overarching theme which is also present in Much Ado About Nothing. Where love is no longer left to chance or the "gods" but is sought after as an end in itself, the price to be paid is that humans become responsible.

Because this is such a different idea from what came before, the presence of the Elder character in the two love stories we have seen makes sense. None of the young people of the time could have had a template for how to go about esoteric love since all of the love stories prior had warned against it. The Elder then becomes the guide towards what was actually a new cultural identity, one that has become normal in our time. That is why the Orphans place themselves in the hands of the Elder. Claudio trusts Don Pedro entirely to organise the marriage with Hero, and then Hero and the others later agree to follow Friar Francis' plan to save the day. Although both Romeo and Juliet are responsible for their decisions and pursue their goal with their own willpower, they rely on Friar Lawrence to come up with the plan. We see this in Romeo's initial meeting with the Friar and then later when Juliet turns to him for help after having been ordered by her father to marry Paris. She demands he solve the problem or she will kill herself:-

Tell me not, Friar, that thou hearest of this,
Unless thou tell me how I may prevent it.
If in thy wisdom thou canst give no help,
Do thou but call my resolution wise,
And with this knife I'll help it presently.

The role of Elder, as we have defined it, is to guide the Orphan towards membership of an institution of society. But that is only the exoteric side of the equation. The Christian priest was the one who consecrated the union of a couple and therefore fulfilled the exoteric role of Elder. What is different in the two love stories we have seen is that the Elder role extends towards helping the young couple esoterically. As the parents relax their mandate over their children's marriage arrangements, the Elder is called in to provide the necessary guidance where young hearts may go off the rails. Don Pedro manages to do that in Much Ado, albeit after a major misstep. Friar Lawrence fails because he doesn't believe in esoteric love in the first place.

The result is that Romeo and Juliet do not have a guide that successfully gets them to holy state at the end of the story. They never manage to find an exoteric identity that matches the esoteric. They never graduate from the Orphan phase of life into a mature Adult identity. In fact, all of the Orphans in the story meet the same fate, including Tybalt and Paris. The larger archetypal dynamic we see right from the first scene is that the story is full of young people without guidance; Orphans without Elders. Lawrence's failure in relation to Romeo and Juliet is mirrored in the failure of their parents and even Prince Escalus in not providing a pathway to adulthood for their young people. Without an exoteric guiding hand, the esoteric is allowed to flow unchecked. The older generation fails to initiate the younger. The failure to return to holy state is true of Romeo and Juliet as individuals; their relationship with each other and their parents; and that between the younger generation and the older in Verona. The breakdown of the microcosmic transformation mirrors the macrocosmic.

It is crucial to understand that none of this is a negation of esoteric love. In fact, the nature of Shakespearean tragedy is to foreground and thereby to venerate the esoteric journey of his heroes. What we celebrate in Romeo and Juliet is the intensity of their love, the sacrifice they are prepared to make for it, and the consciousness with which they approach that sacrifice. Friar Lawrence is the source of "wisdom", but wisdom views this kind of love as foolish. It hearkens back to the point we made about Much Ado. The fact that Romeo and Juliet are young and "foolish" is not a criticism at all. In fact,

Shakespeare makes clear in the final scene that the blame lies with the elders in the story.

Since the rest of the stories we are going to examine in this book are all tragedies (with the big exception of The Tempest), it is worthwhile in conclusion to understand a little more about the nature of how Shakespeare utilises the tragic form. All of Shakespeare's tragic heroes die, and this relates back to the point we made about death and transformation in the introduction.

Because we have defined identity in the widest possible terms to include the biological-familial, the economic, the political, and the religious, we may ask the question: how does death transform each of these? Our personal biological identity ends with death but may be said to live on through our progeny. The same goes for our economic and political identities, which have the potential to carry on outside of our immediate family to the extent that we have contributed to the institutions of society and ensured their propagation. In the esoteric realm, our ideas and our influence may live on through the culture of which we were a part. Finally, there is the ultimate esoteric realm that deals with concepts like the soul or spirit and what happens to them. Most cultures believe something of this lives on after the death of our body, although Shakespeare studiously avoids such questions in his work.

Death may be said to be holy in that it brings an end to life, while life is always sacred in the sense that it is open-ended, irrational, always changing, always becoming. Philosophers and theologians since time immemorial have attempted to define the flux of life and thereby render it into a knowable holy state of reason and logic. But life regularly thumbs its nose at such attempts. At the individual level, while we are alive, we are always changing and therefore always transforming. There are countless mini-transformations within a human life, but life itself is one whole transformation. Death is the holy state that ends all the transformations of life.

If life is always sacred and the sacred state is always about the search for holiness, then it follows that what we do in life is always a striving after something. Because the sacred is full of risk, uncertainty, and ambiguity, we never fully know what we are searching for. The truth of our actions always supersedes our conscious understanding of them. There is something more than just intellect and consciousness at play. We might call it the will. Because a tragedy ends while the hero is still striving for that which they do not fully comprehend, we catch the hero not in the holy state of consciousness but in the sacred state of will. In Shakespeare, the tragic hero dies, sacrificing themselves for that which they are striving towards.

Every Shakespearean tragedy reveals to us the hero in their fullness, both in the sense that they have willed the journey they have taken and in the sense that the full consequences of their sacrifice have become known to them. Thus, we have Macbeth's lament that life is but a poor player who struts his hour on the stage and is seen no more. We have Othello's tragic conflict between love and duty, mixed with the intense guilt of having been fooled by Iago. We have Romeo and Juliet dying in each other's arms. In the final scene, each of these heroes must face the sacrifice they have made in its fullest magnitude. But each of them also consummates that final sacrifice. For Macbeth, it is to go down fighting even though he knows defeat is certain. For Othello, Romeo, and Juliet, it is committing suicide in the name of love. These are not rational decisions. They are born of something deeper. It is that deeper conviction, will, and striving which Shakespeare captures in his tragedies.

This does not mean that Shakespeare has no conception of truth. On the contrary, we may argue that he wishes to expand our understanding of truth. Shakespeare's heroes always attain clarity by the end of the story. Perhaps more importantly, so too do the other characters who are left to pick up the pieces after the truth of all that has happened comes to light. What does this mean?

One of the things it means is that the secrets hidden beneath the actions of the hero come to light alongside all the consequences of their actions. The esoteric truths of the hero, until now cloudy and opaque, become clear and understood. Even though the hero may die, the story ends in a holy state illuminated by this truth. It is not a logical, general, or universal truth; it is the esoteric truth about the individuals involved. It is a revelation of their full identity. That revelation comes to both the hero and, most importantly, to a witness who watches their final moments.

We can be certain of the importance that Shakespeare laid on this truth since the final scene of Hamlet features this exact scenario. Horatio is the witness to Hamlet's journey, but he wants to kill himself due to the grief over what has happened. The dying prince demands that he live on in order to share his story:-

O good Horatio, what a wounded name,
(Things standing thus unknown) shall live behind me.
If thou didst ever hold me in thy heart,
Absent thee from felicity awhile,
And in this harsh world draw thy breath in pain,
To tell my story.

The witness redeems the hero by bringing their esoteric and exoteric identities into alignment. He also becomes the storyteller, making public what had previously only been private.

The power of the unforgettable ending to Romeo and Juliet lies in that the two lovers are each other's witnesses prior to their deaths. But it is only Friar Lawrence who understands what has happened and can therefore provide the exoteric balance. He is given the task of storyteller. This is fitting not only in the practical sense that only he knows the esoteric truths of Romeo and Juliet's love but also because he is the Elder who failed to guide the Orphans through their transformation. By sharing the truth in the final scene, he also makes the older generation aware of their share of the blame.

Romeo and Juliet are not guilty of hubris. They do not presume an identity that is forbidden them; they are already in it. They are already in love, and, of course, they are already married since Friar Lawrence conducts the ceremony himself. What brings them undone is the failure of their family and the wider society to recognise the truth. By finally sharing that truth, Lawrence brings the esoteric and exoteric into alignment. In doing so, he creates the holy state that ends the story.

Hamlet

We have seen several examples of how the distinction between the esoteric and exoteric poles of existence helps to make sense of a number of issues across what are normally considered discrete domains. For example, we have noted that the difference between honour and pride is about the outward-facing and inward-facing manifestations of our identity. We have seen the difference between esoteric love and the exoteric institution of marriage as the propagation of the family, with economic and political considerations being paramount in the latter. We have described how the split between the esoteric and exoteric poles of identity triggers the crisis that every hero must face and how the necessity to reunify the poles guides their journey. Finally, we have described how Shakespeare builds the distinction between the esoteric and exoteric into the very structure of his works by his use of covert exposition to fill out the backstory of the hero, in contrast to the standard form of exposition which is delivered overtly via narration or the words and thoughts of the characters. We might very well say that Shakespeare tells his stories in an esoteric fashion, requiring us to fill in the gaps in our own minds rather than take what is presented to us on stage as the whole truth.

Until now, the covert exposition Shakespeare uses has been straightforward. The backstories of Claudio, Hero, Benedick, Beatrice, Romeo, and Juliet have all been fairly easy to decipher. It's also true that a failure to grasp the backstory of those characters does not prevent an understanding of the main themes in the two plays in question, and that's why there has not been widespread confusion about either Much Ado or Romeo and Juliet. That is not the case with the work to which we now turn, and it is no coincidence that Shakespeare creates in Hamlet an incredibly complex backstory without which it is not possible to grasp the meaning of the work. The error of all the great minds who have tackled Hamlet is that they have only paid attention to what is exoterically shown to them. That is why many of them concluded that the work itself must be flawed.

The technical reason why a failure to understand the covert backstory leads to an incorrect interpretation is because the structure of a story involves a transition out of holy state and into sacred state. If we do not grasp the starting holy state, we also miss the identity crisis that signals the transition to the sacred. Without that, we cannot understand the nature of the sacrifice that the hero is making, and we do not comprehend their motivations for taking the journey in the first place. In relation to Hamlet, when we first meet the prince at the start of the play, he is already well into sacred state. Unless we retrace the events that have led him to his current situation, we simply cannot grasp his transformation to any degree of accuracy, and we misunderstand the story as a result. Therefore, the first task in our analysis will be to unpack the covert exposition that Shakespeare creates in the opening scene of the story. This will unlock the deeper meanings in Hamlet that have gone unnoticed for four centuries.

The timeline of events that forms the backstory is really quite easy to decipher. What we must do is to pause and consider the ramifications of what happens. The starting point for everything is clear: Hamlet's father dies. If there were nothing else to it, this would be a major event in the life of a young man. The death of a loved one initiates the grieving process, which is one of the primary sacred states we all must deal with in the course of life. The death of a father is always a major blow, but we know that Hamlet loved his father. It is made clear throughout the story that he thought the world of the late king. Moreover, Hamlet is a young man living the carefree lifestyle of a student at university. The shock of the news, the need to travel home for the funeral, and the need to make sense of the death – all of these are what Hamlet must go through. This is the first way in which Hamlet is already in sacred state when the story begins. The death of the king takes place two months prior to the start of the action, but it is clear that Hamlet has not ended his grieving.

It is an extraordinary fact that seemingly none of the most famous commentators on Hamlet have understood that what is being shown to us is the grieving process of a young man at the death of his father. Rather, they have fixated on the dramatic twist that comes with the appearance of the ghost, which turns a natural death into a murder. But Hamlet only finds out about the ghost in Act 1, Scene 4 of the play. Even though the murder theme introduces more complexity into proceedings, including via the motif of revenge, which has been given massively overweighted importance, much of the story is not about murder or revenge. It is a meditation on death itself. This is true of two of the most famous scenes. The to-be-or-not-to-be soliloquy is a reflection on death perfectly befitting a sharp young mind that is attempting to make sense of it. Then there is the gravedigger scene where Hamlet marvels at what remains of even the greatest of men when they leave this mortal coil. "To what base uses we may return, Horatio!" Such ruminations on the higher meanings of life are a natural part of the grieving process. All the way until the end of the story, Hamlet is still trying to make sense of death. Therefore, he is still grieving. This is the bedrock of the transformation he is going through, and it begins two months prior to the action that starts the play.

Not only that, the question of grief sits at the heart of the first interaction between Hamlet and his mother in the opening court scene of the story. The scene begins with a ceremonial entrance, Gertrude and Claudius taking the throne, and Hamlet joining the other courtiers. We see that Hamlet is not happy, and he is wearing his official mourning clothes. Claudius announces to the court that the official period of mourning for the former king is now over. He and Gertrude then chastise Hamlet for continuing to mourn longer than is acceptable. Hamlet's mother then asks her son what is quite an extraordinary question: "Why is it so personal to you"? What sort of mother asks her son why the death of his father is "personal"? Hamlet retorts:-

But I have that within, which passeth show;
These, but the trappings and suits of woe.

The prince is telling his mother that he is not pretending. His clothing and demeanour are a reflection of his inner feelings. He is wearing the suits of woe because they reflect how he is within. It should not surprise us by now to find that the dynamic we are shown once again rests on the distinction between the esoteric and the exoteric. In fact, this particular difference is built into the semantics of the English language. It's the contrast between mourning and grieving. The former is the public expression that includes whatever rites and ceremonies a culture practises on the death of an individual. Since Hamlet's father was the king, there is an elaborate formal mourning process which serves not only emotional or psychological purposes but political ones too. People who had never known the king personally would nevertheless be expected to participate by attending the funeral, wearing appropriate clothing, and generally following the accepted customs. The exoteric forms of mourning can be contrasted with the esoteric nature of grieving, which is the personal experience we have when we lose that which we love.

Now, it's rather an obvious fact that the death of a political figure usually involves a mourning process that is decoupled from grieving for the simple reason that the vast majority of people have no connection with a king and never know them personally. Many of the former king's subjects could not have really grieved him, and nobody would hold that against them as long as they did their duty in taking part in the mourning ceremonies. But the question here is not about subjects who didn't know the king; it is about the king's son, his wife, and his uncle. Thus, the initial interaction between Hamlet, Gertrude, and Claudius is highly revealing. Gertrude and Claudius are interested only in the official mourning period. Now that it is over, they are getting on with life. Gertrude's question about the death being "personal" shows that she apparently has no conception of an esoteric process that is separated from the spectacle of mourning. She genuinely doesn't understand what's wrong with Hamlet. Because Gertrude does not feel grief, it follows that she never really loved her late husband.

Thus, Shakespeare makes crystal clear at the very beginning of the play that one of the differences between Hamlet and the other characters in the story is his esoteric love and grief for his father. Many scenes in the story are about this either directly or tangentially. Hamlet's anger at his mother is at least partly grounded in the fact that she does not grieve for her former husband. That is why she is able to remarry so quickly. The famous bedroom scene involves Hamlet comparing the former king and his brother and asking his mother how she could swap a man of virtue for one of vice. Does she not know the difference? This relates to the theme we have already mentioned several times, which is that aristocratic and royal marriages in this era were not done for love but for political purposes. It's actually not that surprising that Gertrude never loved the late king. This leads to another implication. Hamlet was not aware of that. He believed his mother loved his father. The death of the king is teaching him something about how the world works, something he would rather not know.

All of this would be a major challenge for a young prince to deal with. At a very difficult time in life, Hamlet has no support from those who are closest to him. However, Shakespeare adds a series of factors which have the effect of magnifying the challenge. Firstly, it is clear that Hamlet's father was not expected to die. He was neither weak nor sick leading up to the fateful event. On the contrary, he was in the prime of his life. We hear of a recent victory he won over Norway and another one over England. The fact that Hamlet could go off to university rather than stay to serve the kingdom implies peace and stability. Because Hamlet is only a young man, we can infer that his father was in middle age. The grief that Hamlet feels must certainly have been magnified by the fact that this was an untimely death.

In addition, the man who has died was a king. That has all kinds of political and social ramifications. It throws the entire nation into sacred state. Remember, the sacred is synonymous with danger and risk. The death of a king creates the uncertainty that comes with a power vacuum. In the first court scene, we hear that the young prince of Norway, Fortinbras, intends to use this weakened state to try and invade Denmark. It is because of the uncertainty that follows the king's death that Claudius is able to take power in the first place. Something is rotten in the state of Denmark because the death of a king opens up avenues of attack for enemies both within and without.

But the two most important intensifiers are direct and personal for Hamlet.

Hamlet is the heir to the throne of Denmark. We know from the dialogue in the story that both Hamlet and Laertes expected him to be king. Ever since he was a child, Hamlet must have been told that one day he would need to take over from his father. He would have received specific education and training for that purpose. His father very likely gave him direct advice or told stories to give him an idea of how it all worked. Of course, he would have been in and around the court and would have seen it with his own eyes. On the announcement of his father's death, Hamlet would have expected to be named the next king. But that did not happen. Claudius has taken the throne instead. Although, technically, Hamlet was not guaranteed the throne due to the nature of the Danish elector system, it is a slap in the face when his uncle is named king instead of himself. It is both a personal affront and a clue that something shady is going on.

That leads to the final intensifier, which is the remarriage of Gertrude to Claudius. At a personal level, this means Hamlet now has a stepfather who is also his uncle. That would be bad enough, but it is clear Hamlet has little to no respect for Claudius. Not only that, Hamlet has to deal with the remarriage of his mother to his uncle while he is still grieving for his late father. Imagine how he must feel when both Gertrude and Claudius refer to the new king as Hamlet's "father" on several occasions. The play was written at a time when divorce was unheard of and remarriage rare. But, in the modern world, we have no trouble recognising the psychology that comes from the arrival of a step-parent. Then add in the fact that the stepfather is also the uncle, and the wonder is not that Hamlet is upset but that he's not more upset.

All of these intensifiers are present before the action of the play even begins. They are part of the covert exposition that Shakespeare creates, and they have received little to no attention from commentators. The event that has drawn all the attention is the one that is shown early on in the story. The ghost of the dead king appears firstly to the nightwatchmen and then to Hamlet. For some reason, the ghost has become synonymous with Hamlet's need to get revenge against his uncle. When we pay attention to what the ghost actually says, however, we find that, although it does briefly mention revenge in its first discussion with the prince, its main concern is that Hamlet should guide his mother towards some kind of redemption for her behaviour. The ghost explicitly says that Hamlet is not to seek revenge against her, which is precisely what Gertrude later expects in the famous bedroom scene. Her fear that Hamlet has come to kill her is what causes Polonius to blow his cover. Gertrude is expecting that Hamlet has come to atone for the honour of his father because both she and Claudius have tarnished it through their actions, irrespective of their guilt over his murder. What she cannot comprehend, and what most commentators have missed, is that Hamlet has an esoteric plan in mind. He is not there for revenge but redemption.

Putting all this together, we have what is perhaps the most complete and total identity crisis in any of Shakespeare's stories. All of the aspects of Hamlet's identity have been called into question. Most importantly, his identity crisis occurs before the action of the story begins. Even the revenge motif has its origins earlier on because we learn from the first encounter with the ghost that Hamlet already had his suspicions about Claudius. This makes perfect sense. His otherwise healthy father dies suddenly while nobody else is around, and then Claudius unexpectedly takes the throne. When that kind of thing happens in the corridors of power, it is only natural to suspect foul play. Hamlet may be young and relatively inexperienced, but he is no fool. On the contrary, he is one of the brightest minds in all literature.

Now that we have sketched the outlines of the main theme of the story and the way in which it is set up via covert exposition, let's walk back through the events as Hamlet must have experienced them so that we can be very clear about his starting holy state and the transition into the sacred that begins with the death of the king.

The holy state for Hamlet finds him in the Orphan stage of life. He has already made a separation from his parents by travelling away from home to attend university in Wittenberg. Hamlet's identity as university student is complemented by his biological-familial identity as the son to a noble and distinguished father and a seemingly virtuous mother. Of course, he is also the heir to the throne of Denmark, meaning that Hamlet would fully expect to one day be king. In this respect, Hamlet is highly unusual because his holy state is not just the stable Orphan identity of his current situation but a future

Adult identity that is already mapped out for him and which he would have been told about for his entire childhood. What is going to be destroyed is not just the various aspects of his identity but his understanding of what the future holds and the entire worldview he has been raised with as a child.

We are now able to imagine the magnitude of the transition from holy state to sacred state. Hamlet would have been at university when a messenger delivered the news that his father had died. He would drop everything and travel immediately to the German coast to get the next available ship back home. Most likely, the trip would include long delays and plenty of time to think about what had happened. As a loving son, the loss of his father would have been foremost in his mind. But alongside this loss and the grief that comes with it, more practical matters would also have elbowed their way into his consciousness. Hamlet was the son and heir, meaning he was now the inheritor of his father's estate. He would now be a land owner, which would bring with it various responsibilities. Of course, the overwhelmingly more important consideration is that he would expect to be named king in the months ahead. That means his time at university is over; his carefree, fun-loving lifestyle of a student is gone and will be replaced by the highest responsibility of all, leading the nation of Denmark.

Because Hamlet is an only child and seems to have no cousins, close relations, or even close friends (Rosencrantz and Guildenstern betray him later in the story), the main person he would expect to share his grief with is his mother. Hamlet might expect that his mother will be just as distraught as he is. Once again, practical matters would also need to be considered. Since she is now without a husband, there would need to be arrangements made about Gertrude's future. A relevant cultural issue here is that Denmark had some of the more favourable laws for widows at this time. Gertrude would almost certainly own some property and enjoy a degree of independence. Her later decision to remarry must be understood against this background. There could be no question that she was doing it for economic reasons, especially because her son was almost certain to become king.

These were the thoughts that must have been swirling around the young prince's mind on the boat journey back home. Eventually, Hamlet would have arrived home and travelled to the castle at Elsinore. The period of mourning would have been underway, and there would have been the official ceremonies and rites pertaining to the death of a king, including the public funeral, and so on. For these events, Hamlet, Gertrude, Claudius, and the other dignitaries would have to play the role assigned to them by convention. They would have to put on the mask of mourning. But we know from the dramatic exchange in the opening scene that Hamlet is also grieving. Crucially, he is the only one doing so. When we imagine him on the boat travelling home, we must imagine that he is primarily trying to come to terms with the death of his father. Then, he arrives home. What does he find? He finds a whole host of exoteric ceremonies. He finds mourning, but he does not find grief, including and especially in the people he should expect it from the most: his mother and uncle. As a young man in the Orphan stage of life, Hamlet is the one who needs counselling and guidance, and he should get it from those who have more experience. But he gets nothing; nothing from Gertrude, nothing from Claudius, nothing from Polonius or any of the other courtiers.

The realisation must have occurred to Hamlet shortly after arriving home: nobody else is grieving. Nobody cares about the death of his father except himself. There is a wonderful vignette later in the story on this subject. In the banter between Hamlet and Ophelia before the start of the play which the prince has set up as a trap for his uncle, Hamlet deliberately gets the date of his father's death wrong. Ophelia corrects him, proving that she remembers it. He playfully remarks that this at least proves that a great king will be remembered for at least four months after he is gone.

Hamlet's isolation, which is a feature of the story, must have begun very shortly after arriving back in Denmark. He begins to see for the first time in his life what the court really is: that it is populated by automatons who are just going through the motions. Their obedience to the dead king was motivated not by genuine respect or love but by mechanical duty. The sardonic attitude we see displayed by the prince towards Polonius later in the story must be born out of the bitterness that Hamlet felt watching the old man and the other courtiers wearing the mask of mourning without any of the actual grief that would come with genuine feelings of affection.

We know from the facts of the story that the mourning period lasts for two months. During that time, Hamlet would have been stewing on these considerations, forced to go through the empty rituals knowing that nobody else really cared. The end of the mourning period would coincide with the appointment of the next king within the Danish system of elective monarchy. Up until this point, Hamlet has no reason to suspect that his uncle had been drumming up support from the courtiers to get himself elected king. As the eldest son, Hamlet is the default choice and would have assumed to be nominated. Due to his grieving and the cynicism he must have been feeling towards the courtiers, it seems likely Hamlet would not have actively tried to confirm that he was favoured to be king. Perhaps he did and was brushed off. In any case, the council eventually makes its announcement, unexpectedly naming Claudius.

Imagine you are Hamlet. You have come home grieving for your dead father. You have quickly realised that nobody in the court shares your grief. They are just going through the officially required motions of mourning. Incredibly, you realise that your own mother and uncle are doing the same. You are not just dealing with grief over your father but with a much larger kind of grief, namely, the loss of some key planks of your worldview. Your mother is not who you thought she was. Neither is your uncle. You start to see court politics for what it really is, and it sickens you. Then, the very same courtiers who have been making a great show of mourning name your uncle as king instead of you. You realise that the façade of mourning did not just hide a lack of grief; it hid a deceitful political operation being conducted at your expense. Where grief should have been, there was instead only greed, ambition and cunning. You start to wonder whether the same greed, ambition, and cunning could have been behind the death of your otherwise perfectly healthy father.

And then, just when things could seemingly get no worse, you find out that your mother and uncle are going to marry. The same two people who have also been feigning grief for the last few weeks are now hoisted upon the throne by the same cunning political calculations that have prevented your ascension. A truly horrifying thought must have occurred to Hamlet at this point: could his own mother have been involved in the death of his father? This is the plot of the famous Greek myth of Clytemnestra murdering Agamemnon and then marrying Aegisthus, after which the two became king and queen. It cannot be a coincidence that the ghost later takes the trouble to confirm that Gertrude was innocent of the death of the king. The thought must have occurred to Hamlet.

The sequence we have just laid out occurs prior to the beginning of the play. In fact, the final gut-wrenching revelation comes in one fell swoop just before the start of the action. Hamlet would have found out all at once that he was not to be king, that his uncle would take the throne instead, and that his mother would join him. This coincided with the end of the mourning period two months after the death of his father. It would have been the first time Hamlet wondered whether that death had been intentional.

We can see now that the young prince begins the play not just in sacred state but in one of the most intense sacred states imaginable. His entire worldview has been shattered. His picture of a just and noble kingdom led by a wise king is gone. Around him are only people who seem like actors in a bad play. Hamlet's familial identity has been rocked, his political identity thrown into limbo, his future rendered unknowable. A.C. Bradley called this "melancholy". No, it is an existential crisis of the first order, and the marvel is that Hamlet is not far more shaken than he is. In the circumstances, he is a model of clarity and resolve.

Incredibly, there is still one more element to add to the implied backstory that Shakespeare creates by covert exposition: the love between Hamlet and Ophelia. It must be the case that their relationship began in the weeks before the start of the action since both Polonius and Laertes treat the news of it at the start of the play as a surprise. This may seem to contradict our previous assertion that Hamlet is going through an existential crisis, but, again, the timing here is crucial. The full nature of that crisis only happens with the announcement that Claudius is taking the throne. Up until that point, Hamlet may have been severely disillusioned with the lack of grief over his dead father, but he would still have expected to be named king and would be readying himself for that eventuality. If that's true, then he finds himself in a very similar position to Claudio in Much Ado About Nothing. He expects his Adult political identity to be secured very shortly. The time is right to start looking for a queen.

This element of the covert exposition also helps to explain another seemingly minor detail of the opening court scene. Laertes wants to return to university and goes out of his way to achieve that outcome. When Hamlet is denied the same opportunity, he puts up no resistance whatsoever. Since his relationship with Ophelia was still blossoming at this time, staying around the castle gives him the opportunity to spend time with her. That is certainly the real reason behind his acquiescence to his uncle's request.

If that's true, then the scene that immediately follows also takes on far greater significance than it would otherwise. Before leaving for Paris, Laertes warns Ophelia away from Hamlet by telling her that she is not in contention to become queen and, therefore, nothing can come of their relationship except a loss of her honour. Given that Ophelia becomes a reclusive and depressed figure later in the story, it is important to note that she is bright and cheerful in this opening scene. She easily brushes aside her brother's advice by pointing out that he's a hypocrite who counsels her towards virtue while himself being a "puff'd and reckless libertine". We see here is that Ophelia is more than happy with the situation and won't be dissuaded by Laertes. That makes what happens next even more important.

Ophelia's father, Polonius, has overhead the conversation between his son and daughter. It turns out that he is already aware of the court gossip about Hamlet and Ophelia. He demands to know what is going on. When Ophelia says it is all perfectly honourable, Polonius replies that Hamlet is young and has more freedom of action than she does. To protect her honour, he forbids her from any further contact with the prince. Although it is clear that this is upsetting for her, Ophelia says she will obey.

Not only will this later prove to be ruinous for Ophelia, it is yet another blow for Hamlet who has now had his crown and his queen taken away. His political and his familial identities, which must have seemed rock solid just days earlier, go up in smoke. The bitter irony is that the freedom that Hamlet has, which Polonius uses as the justification to force Ophelia away from him, only exists because Polonius (inadvertently) helped Claudius steal the crown. Were that not the case, the very same conversation would take on a drastically different tone because it would not be a free Hamlet who had fallen for Ophelia; it would be a King Hamlet. In those circumstances, even a dullard like Polonius would be smart enough to count his lucky stars and seek to have the marriage between his daughter and the new king arranged as quickly as possible.

To say it again, Hamlet's identity crisis is complete in the sense that it affects all the elements of his being. The death of his father ends the Orphan phase of life and should have thrust him forward into the Adult archetype as king. Not only has that not occurred, he has been thrown back into something far more like childhood, stuck in the castle in Elsinore with no official position, trapped under the eternal surveillance of the court with not even his love for Ophelia to console him. What begins as grief for his father turns into a much more general kind of grief for his lost identity and the worldview that upheld it, which now appears to him only in the illusory form of a ghost at midnight.

Grief occurs when we lose that which we love. Where there is nobody to blame, we must try and make sense of the loss, which usually triggers larger questions about the meaning of life. It is a different thing when there is a guilty party. The grieving process must still continue because we have still lost something, but it now comes with feelings of anger. This is where the issue of revenge enters the equation. The question that has puzzled seemingly all commentators is why Hamlet does not take revenge on Claudius for his actions. These commentators have simply not even realised that Hamlet is grieving, and they write off all the elements in the story which show us that by saying that it is nothing more than "melancholy". These invalid conclusions are the result of their failure to understand covert exposition.

But there is a much larger problem with the revenge motif that doesn't even require an understanding of the bigger picture. The only evidence that Hamlet has that his father was murdered has come from a ghost. Imagine that some of the great thinkers and philosophers have all watched the play and concluded that Hamlet absolutely should kill his uncle in cold blood based on nothing more than the testimony of a strange apparition in the night! Even setting aside what we now know of the backstory, there are a number of problems with this whole way of thinking. Firstly, as we have already noted, the ghost does not tell Hamlet to seek revenge. In fact, the only explicit instruction it gives is that he should lead his mother towards contrition for her actions and that he should do so without hurting her. If anything, the ghost can be seen to be asking him not to engage in violence.

The second problem is more important, and it is the one that Hamlet himself remarks upon. How can he trust the advice given by a ghost in the middle of the night? Apart from anything else, if he has to explain why he has just killed his uncle, can he say "a ghost told me to"? Would any reasonable person think that was a sane and justifiable reason to commit cold-blooded murder? The answer is, of course, no. Yet the position of learned thinkers has been that Hamlet should just take the ghost's word for it and do his uncle in. Not only does that not make sense, Hamlet himself meditates on this exact problem. He doesn't write the ghost off altogether; rather, he comes up with a much better plan, one that any philosopher must agree with. He's going to get proof that the ghost is correct by laying a trap for Claudius:-

I know my course. The spirit that I have seen
May be the Devil, and the Devil hath power
T'assume a please shape, yea and perhaps
Out of my weakness, and my melancholy,
As he is very potent with such spirits,
Abuses me to damn me. I'll have grounds
More relative than this: the play's the thing.
Wherein I'll catch the conscience of the King. (Act 2, Scene 2)

This passage alone should have put an end to the idea that Hamlet's failure to kill Claudius is driven by melancholy. Hamlet knows that he is feeling melancholic. Why? Because he is still grieving over the death of his father. He is fully aware that the state he is in makes him "weak" and liable to be deceived by visions which assume a pleasing shape. The ghost is telling him what he wants to hear. That's the sort of thing the devil might do. Suggesting that you kill your uncle in cold blood without evidence is also the kind of thing the devil would say. We must remember that the appearance of the ghost comes right after Claudius steals the throne. It was the exact time when Hamlet would have come to the shocking realisation of what had really been going on, and, of course, his suspicions about whether Claudius and even Gertrude were involved in the death of his father must have been raging. Then he sees a ghost who tells him what he has already been thinking. When Macbeth is told what he wants to hear by the three witches, he ends up murdering his king in cold blood. When Hamlet is told what he is already thinking, he stops and questions the veracity of the information. He is not doing that out of cowardice or softness; he is doing it out of self-awareness. Far from being a sign of weakness, this shows incredible strength of mind and a philosophical understanding that matches Socrates and Descartes, who also knew how easy it was to fool oneself. Hamlet is not going to be fooled like Macbeth.

More than that, the above proves that Hamlet is not procrastinating at all. He simply does not share the implied goal of revenge that has been imposed upon him by others. What he is doing instead is gathering evidence. He wants to prove that his uncle really is guilty. The ghost has told him so, but Hamlet wants something more concrete than strange visions in the night. Let's put it in more abstract terms. Hamlet is seeking truth and justice. What's more, this goal is entirely of his own making. The ghost doesn't tell him to seek truth and justice. Nobody else does either. It is a task that Hamlet sets for himself, knowing full well that those around him would not even understand it, let alone support him in his mission. That is Hamlet's response to his identity crisis. He deliberately decides not to pursue revenge without it being grounded in truth.

All of this would be laudable enough, but it is also clearly the best course of action from a broader political and social standpoint. Shakespeare shows us in Macbeth what happens when the transfer of political power is achieved by violence. For Hamlet to simply kill Claudius would be even more likely to lead to problems because at least Macbeth takes the trouble to create an alibi. Moreover, if we think about how Claudius achieved his rise to the top, it was not done with an act of violence but with what is clearly a well-planned and well-executed operation that killed the king in a way that looked accidental and then stitched up the numbers behind the scenes. Claudius went out of his way to ensure that his election to the throne had all the appearance of legitimacy. That is why he was able to get away with it. That's also why Hamlet cannot simply kill him without first destroying the perceived legitimacy.

However, it is clear that Hamlet is not thinking primarily about the political angle. His search for truth and justice is his response to the existential crisis that he faces. It is his answer to the grieving process. Just as Hamlet had to grieve alone at the time when everybody else was only mourning, he must seek the truth alone at a time when everybody else has simply gotten on with their lives as if nothing had happened. Thus, far from being a melancholic procrastinator, as most critics have claimed, Hamlet has actually constructed for himself a plan of attack and is putting it into action. Moreover, the plan is quite fitting to the circumstances. Claudius killed the king in a secret, esoteric fashion. This requires an esoteric response. It would be a completely different matter if the former king had been obviously murdered. Then, Hamlet would have been well within his rights to take up arms against the culprit. Shakespeare reinforces this by making it the exact plotline later on when Polonius is killed accidentally. How does Laertes respond? He storms the castle and is on the verge of killing Claudius. Hamlet never had the opportunity to try this because by the time he arrived home, all of the court, including his own mother and uncle, were following the narrative that had been created about an accidental death. Even if Hamlet had suspected something at that time, there was nothing he could do within the bounds of propriety.

Of course, none of this leads to a happy outcome. As brilliant and laudable as Hamlet's plan is, it ultimately fails, and it does so for much the same reasons as Romeo and Juliet's, namely, that Hamlet's pursuit of the esoteric goals of truth and justice never finds exoteric manifestation. If we think about it, Hamlet is in an even worse position than the star-crossed lovers. At least Juliet's parents were open to the esoteric side of life and even encouraged it in their daughter. Hamlet is entirely trapped within the exoteric machine of the Danish court. His attempts to spark the conscience of his own mother ultimately fail, and there is even less likelihood of success with Polonius or the other dim-witted courtiers. How could esoteric truth take hold in such an environment?

But this is not entirely correct. There was at least one character with whom Hamlet was able to interact on the esoteric level, and that was Ophelia. Who was it that put a stop to that? Polonius. Meanwhile, we can see from the jesting between Hamlet and Rosencrantz and Guildenstern that the three could have been friends. In fact, Hamlet shares with his two contemporaries some of his plan (the fact that he is pretending to be mad) and therefore engages them on the esoteric level. Who spoils that relationship? Claudius. It is also Claudius who later turns Laertes and Hamlet against each other. In fact, the split between the exoteric and esoteric that exists in the story is also a split between generations. What is going on in Hamlet is an intergenerational conflict that was also present in the other two stories we have examined that featured Orphan heroes.

In Romeo and Juliet, the Parents and Elders in the story are mostly negligent. Their failure to usher the Orphans towards a mature Adult identity is not born out of malice or ill will but out of ignorance. They simply don't know the true cause of the trouble or how to fix it. The strange thing is, this is also true of Claudius, Gertrude, and Polonius. Even though Claudius has murdered his father and usurped his throne, it is clear that he does not bear any ill will against Hamlet. If he did, it would be a simple matter to have the prince killed, but Claudius only tries to do that later in the story when he thinks that Hamlet has become dangerous. Even then, Claudius doesn't really understand Hamlet's position. There is a line after Hamlet has accidentally killed Polonius where Claudius says that his nephew has no "deviousness" in him. Claudius doesn't understand his nephew at all. If he did, he would have realised that Hamlet had been devious in the extreme by constructing a false identity as a madman in order to fool him and then putting on a play that was specifically designed to present his crime back to him.

Note that this incomprehension is mutual. The question of why Claudius wanted to rule in the first place is unresolved, as is the reason why Gertrude wanted to remarry. Claudius has none of the Warrior-hatred that we see in Macbeth and Iago. He is a politician, not a fighter. His motives are opaque, as are his methods. As for Gertrude, stability and order seem to be the only values in life for her. Anything which disturbs the peace is a problem. That would explain her decision to marry Claudius. It was a thing she could do to ensure a quick return to perceived harmony. We are invited to believe that everybody else in the court went along with the matter for no other reason than it was the path of least resistance. As long as exoteric appearances are kept up, the older generation is satisfied. They simply have no esoteric attunement to the world.

But more than that, we can see that the behaviour of the older generation is intended to snuff out the esoteric wherever it appears. Polonius is a bore and dullard of the first order. He also smothers his children. He tries to prevent Laertes from returning to university and, when he loses the argument, organises a spy to watch over him. He joins with Claudius to organise Rosencrantz and Guildenstern to spy on Hamlet. He intervenes to destroy Ophelia's happiness with the prince. He himself becomes a spy against Hamlet, an occupation which eventually costs him his life. From the archetypal point of view, the Adults in the story spend their entire time watching over and conspiring against the Orphans, but they do so in a completely unconscious fashion and without any malice. What Shakespeare shows us in Hamlet is a kind of misplaced duty. The parents, who cannot understand their children and, if we are honest, do not really love them, overcompensate by smothering them instead.

There is another crucial implication here. The fact that Hamlet had been allowed to go to university in the first place implies that his father had encouraged his son to develop himself away from home. In other words, he had guided Hamlet into the Orphan phase of life. No sooner is the old king dead than Hamlet is forced back into the castle and finds himself trapped in a stifling domestic situation. A healthy relationship between father and son is replaced by a toxic one between stepfather, mother and son. The death of the old king was also the death of the esoteric, and that is another reason why something is rotten in the state of Denmark.

The exoteric-esoteric split that sits at the heart of the story is therefore also the split between the generations, with the older representing the exoteric and the younger the esoteric. Claudius, Gertrude, and Polonius do not know how to grieve for the dead king because they do not actually have any love for him. Their world is entirely the exoteric world of appearances. They are running on autopilot. The death of a king is a mere blip to be corrected. They simply rearrange things to best ensure the continuation of business as usual. That is why they do not understand Hamlet's grief. It is why they have no understanding of Hamlet and Ophelia's love. Even Claudius' eventual attempt to have Hamlet killed is not part of any larger insight into what is going through the mind of the prince. It is about ensuring that the façade of stability is maintained at all times. It is the absence of esoteric understanding that motivates Polonius and Gertrude to seriously think Hamlet is capable of murdering his mother when just minutes earlier he had all the opportunity and reason to kill Claudius and did not do so. To say it one last time, the older generation simply does not understand the younger.

As for the younger generation, Hamlet is the odd one out because he understands the problem. He knows what was lost with the death of his father and what it has been replaced with. He watched as those in power went through the motions of mourning for the dead king, knowing he was the only one who actually grieved. Then he saw the machinations of the court mindlessly turn to steal the crown from him and give it to a man who is a murderer. The existential crisis that Hamlet has gone through has made him see exoteric authority as disconnected from esoteric substance. His goal throughout the story is to try and reinject the esoteric back into matters in the form of truth and justice. But, one-by-one, those who should have been his allies fall away. Ophelia meekly allows her father to ruin her love with Hamlet. Compare her against Juliet, who is prepared to die rather than give up Romeo. Rosencrantz and Guildenstern side with Claudius against the prince, even when it means sending him to his death. Finally, there is Laertes, who allows himself to be manipulated by Claudius' silver tongue. The only one who remains true to Hamlet is Horatio. But Horatio is in no position to help.

Thus, there is something more than just misunderstanding going on. The older generation may not understand the younger, but they know perfectly well how to keep them divided. But, to say it again, all this happens unconsciously and automatically. It would be one thing if Claudius and

Polonius were like Macbeth and fully admitted to themselves that they just wanted power and didn't care what it cost. But they do not have that level of self-awareness because the esoteric side of their identity is completely lacking. Despite that, they know how to manipulate the esoteric in others. It is fitting that the final scene involves a fight orchestrated by Claudius. Ever the devious politician, the king is going to have somebody else do his dirty work. Note that Laertes has the exact same demand as Hamlet. He wants truth and justice in relation to the death of his father. Claudius knows how to stoke his anger for ulterior purposes, and Laertes lacks the self-awareness and strength of mind of the prince. The final desperate attempt of the older generation to hold onto power ends up killing the younger generation altogether. Just as in Romeo and Juliet, the entire lineages of the families involved are destroyed.

The tragedy is heightened by the fact that Hamlet finally has the thing he has been seeking since the beginning. He has definitive proof of his uncle's wickedness in the form of the letter sent to England with the request to kill the prince. Hamlet had successfully avoided the temptation of violence for the whole play in order to seek truth and justice. It is Laertes' failure to do the same that brings them both undone. Laertes still has faith in exoteric authority.

Hamlet's return to Elsinore at the end gives us a glimpse of the holy state that might have finished the story. The prince is one step away from bringing his father's killer to justice, taking the throne that was rightfully his, and making his mother see the error of her ways. He is vanishingly close to overcoming his identity crisis and becoming the Ruler that he was always destined to be. Fortinbras speculates in the last lines of the play that Hamlet was likely to have made a good king. We don't need to be told that. The whole story has proved beyond doubt that Hamlet would likely have been an even greater Ruler than his father. But as Hamlet himself had to learn in the aftermath of the old king's murder, truth, justice, and virtue are not guaranteed in this world. They arrive briefly and are quickly forgotten afterwards. All we may do is follow the prince's example and strive after them anyway.

Macbeth

We now leave behind the world of the Orphans, their struggles to free themselves of the smothering "love" of their parents, and their valiant efforts to construct meaningful identities in societies that are almost indifferent to their needs. For the rest of the book, our heroes will belong to the Adult world of maturity, discipline, competence, and willpower. This by no means signifies that the heroes in question are good and virtuous. In Macbeth, and especially in Iago, we find Shakespeare's two greatest villains. It is the combination of villainy with the aforementioned virtues of discipline, competence, and willpower that sets them apart as unique characters not just in Shakespeare's *oeuvre* but in stories more generally.

We have already met two villains in our analysis. The first was Don John in Much Ado About Nothing, whose primary motivation was a kind of bored malaise, and whose villainy was of a relatively small magnitude given that nobody was going to die as a result of his actions. The villainy of Hamlet's uncle Claudius was of a much greater magnitude. He has already committed one murder and sought to add a second scalp in the young prince. Ultimately, his actions lead to the ruination of the entire royal line of which he is a part.

Whether Don John felt bad about his actions or repented afterwards is not something we ever find out. Claudius shows signs of a guilty conscience but is unable to repent when he attempts it in the famous scene in the chapel where Hamlet decides not to kill him precisely because he assumes his uncle is seeking salvation, and he doesn't want to consummate it for him. In any case, neither story is an in-depth exploration of villainy for the simple reason that neither of these characters is the hero.

That is not true of the work to which we now turn. Macbeth is Shakespeare's most relentless and brutal portrayal of villainy. Just like Claudius, Macbeth will kill the king in order to take power. Given that the murder of King Hamlet was also premeditated, it may well be that the brilliant portrayal we see in Macbeth of a man wrestling with his conscience before the conduct of a terrible deed is directly applicable to Hamlet's uncle. But the method of the murder is very different because the individuals are very different. Claudius is a politician, and his power lies in his ability to flatter, lie, and deceive. The manner in which he kills the king (poison) has a womanly connotation. In classical mythology, domestic poisoning is always carried out by a bitter wife or other female character. By contrast, Macbeth kills Duncan using a dagger. Daggers were one of the primary weapons of that era wielded by the archetype that Macbeth belongs to: the Warrior. Claudius takes power by deceit and attempts to hold it using the same method. Macbeth ascends to power through violence and holds it briefly in the same way.

Although Claudius and Macbeth are both villains, the nature of their villainy is different in large part because they manifest different archetypes. There is a more general principle at stake here that we can understand using Jung's concept of *the shadow*. We can say that every archetype has its shadow. These are the prototypical vices that come with the job description, so to speak. For a Ruler archetype such as Claudius, lies and deceit are at the top of the list of shadow attributes because it has been known since ancient times that these are the necessary evils of political life. The best a Ruler can hope for is to keep the lies small and harmless. But the line between a little white lie and a campaign of deceit to take the throne of a virtuous king is much thinner than most people would realise. The difference between the archetype and its shadow is not as great as we would hope. In fact, all of Shakespeare's stories feature the hero wrestling with the shadow forms of his or her archetype because the journey into the sacred is what tempts us into the shadow forms in the first place.

Nowhere is that made clearer than in Macbeth. But Macbeth is a Warrior and his temptation is towards the shadow forms of the Warrior archetype. The shadow forms of the Warrior have also been known since ancient times. There are several sections in Plato where the discussion turns to how to prevent the Warrior class as a whole from doing exactly what Macbeth does, which is to steal power from the ruling class. It's not hard to see why this can happen. A Warrior is trained in the martial arts. The more proficient the Warrior, the better they are at, let us say, *neutralising* other people. While the Warrior is neutralising the enemies of the state, everything is fine. But what is to stop him from turning his skills and experience against his own countrymen and extorting them for his own benefit? What is to stop the Warrior from turning his skills against the Ruler and taking power for himself?

Plato's solution was to educate Warriors in philosophy so that they learn to appreciate the finer things in life and to understand virtues. Since Plato believed that the state should be governed according to reason, he thought that giving Warriors training in its use would lead them also to conclude that they should not use force against the governing classes. The logic goes as follows: if society is ruled by nothing else but force, then taking power by force will create the constant need to defend it by force, at which point civilisation collapses into barbarism.

It is exactly this dynamic which Shakespeare explores in the story of Macbeth. There is no evidence that Macbeth is educated in the finer faculties of the philosopher. To the extent that he uses reason at all, it is a faulty kind of reasoning prompted by the superficial truths shown to him by the weird sisters, the three witches and their potent brews. The main battle is not between desire and reason but between desire and conscience. Although Shakespeare does not neglect the exoteric ramifications of Macbeth's bloody theft of power, what distinguishes the story is the esoteric view it gives us of a man who battles against his own conscience. Once the Warrior "defeats" conscience, he gives in to the purest will-to-power. In Hamlet, Claudius is the Shadow Ruler who can at least maintain the appearance of exoteric equilibrium through his deft manipulation of others. As a Warrior, Macbeth has no such subtle arts at his command. His personal abandonment of conscience becomes the governing force of the state, with the wisdom, empathy, and grace of the Ruler lying dead in a pool of blood.

This is a problem that has been around since at least Plato, and modern history shows that it is just as relevant today as it ever was. The great blood baths of the 20th century were ushered in by men who followed in Macbeth's footsteps by either directly or indirectly dethroning a king or emperor and then, when the old authority figure was dead and gone, ruling by brute force alone. Did the butchers of the 20th century also wrestle with their conscience before doing so? The evidence suggests not. What distinguishes Macbeth is that there is nothing inevitable about his descent. On the contrary, what we are presented with at the start of the story is a man who embodies all the virtues of the Warrior in their finest flower. For that reason, Macbeth holds his place as arguably Shakespeare's most tragic character. His fall from grace is both the most rapid and the most destructive.

***

We begin our analysis of the story with our now familiar first task of understanding and describing the holy state of the hero. At first glance, Macbeth seems to follow Hamlet in the sense that we are already in sacred state when the action begins. There is a war on. War is the macrocosmic sacred state where the identity of the nation itself is undergoing a potentially dramatic transformation. War is almost always the result of tensions that have been building over time during what is otherwise a holy state of peace. We see that several thanes have betrayed King Duncan and allied with the Norwegian invaders. The kingdom has been split apart, and the early signs do not suggest that it will survive. Then, Macbeth dramatically swoops in to save the day. He and Banquo almost singlehandedly drive the Norwegians out and leave the traitorous thanes twisting in the wind. The first thing Duncan does after the war is over is to reward the two heroes with the titles of those who have been defeated. The kingdom appears to have ended its own dramatic journey into the sacred and returned to the holy state of peace. Within our model, we could say that the story begins in sacred state and then transitions to holy almost immediately with victory.

However, when we focus on the hero, Macbeth, an argument could be made that all this belongs to his personal holy state. In Shakespeare, as in most of history, political and military conflict is not an aberration but the normal state of affairs. It is the job of the Warrior class to defend society against its enemies. It is the job of the Ruler to reward those who are faithful and punish those who are not. Thus, the opening scenes of the story could very well be said to represent the holy state, the normal and healthy operation of a nation which must always be willing and able to defend itself.

This reading is reinforced by the fact that it is clear that this is not Macbeth's first rodeo. We are not dealing with a neophyte like Claudio in Much Ado About Nothing but an experienced campaigner at the top of his game. Macbeth is already a thane. Although his age is never made explicit, we have every reason to believe he is in mid-life. He equates, therefore, to Don Pedro and Benedick in Much Ado in that he is a career soldier. Note that none of these male characters have children. Macbeth is at least married, but it is his compatriot, Banquo, who has a family. Such facts are never accidental in Shakespeare, and they play an important role in subsequent events in the story.

We might say that the act of fighting war belongs to the holy state of both Macbeth and Banquo in the sense that it is a world they know well and are competent and capable of handling. They are experienced in battle and know how to handle themselves. But there is something special about this particular occasion. It is not Macbeth and Banquo's first battle, but it almost certainly is the first time they have saved the kingdom from defeat. As always, Shakespeare includes in the opening holy state a little scratch that will eventually become a gaping wound. Macbeth's ego has every right to be inflated in the aftermath of a war where he not only snatched victory from the hands of defeat but also saved the kingdom. While he was risking his life on the front lines, King Duncan was safely removed from danger, doing nothing more than waiting for news of the outcome. Who really is the leader of the kingdom in such circumstances? It is not hard to understand why a great Warrior may begin to ask such dangerous questions.

And that is where the three witches come into the picture. Right in the aftermath of the battle, when the glory and exhilaration of victory have not yet dissipated, it is exactly these thoughts that they put into the minds of Macbeth and Banquo by promising both that they are fated to become king.

Banquo laughs the suggestion away as nothing more than silliness, but it is very clear that the weird sisters strike a nerve with Macbeth. Thus, when the news arrives immediately that Duncan has done exactly what he should do as a wise and just Ruler and rewarded the two men who have just saved the kingdom by giving them extra titles as Thanes, rather than put an end to the sacred state of war and return the kingdom and the soldiers back to holy state, this serves instead to begin to transition Macbeth into his own private sacred state as he begins to flirt with the idea of becoming Ruler himself.

There is a crucial factor in this opening scene, one that most people are likely to miss, and one that leads us to infer that King Duncan may not ever have been a Warrior himself. Duncan decides to spend the evening immediately after the battle at Macbeth's estate. Nominally, this may seem like a good idea. It is another reward for Macbeth's bravery. It is a way to bring the difficult period of conflict to an end and strengthen ties with the man who has just proved himself the best Warrior in the kingdom. But, in fact, it comes far too close at the end of the battle, and it serves not to bring the war to an end but to bring the war directly to Duncan himself.

We now know how to understand this because, if war is a transformation, then it also has a starting holy state (peace), a sacred state (battle), and a concluding holy state (peace). Clearly, the actual fighting represents the sacred state. How, then, does the return to the holy state at the end of a war occur? In actual fact, the process is a lot more complex than most people realise. It usually begins with an armistice, an agreement to stop fighting and pursue peace, various negotiations leading to a peace treaty, and then the carrying out of whatever steps have been agreed to. Along the way, the fighting forces need to be demobilised, and there is the potentially difficult process of transitioning back into civilian life. All soldiers who were involved in the sacred state of battle must make the transition back to holy state of peace; that includes Macbeth and Banquo.

Seemingly all societies have a number of ceremonies and rites that pertain to both the beginning and end of a war. In our terminology, these rites facilitate the transition out of the holy state of peace into the sacred state of battle and then back again. These ceremonies and rites serve political and social purposes, but they also assist the Warriors themselves to make the transition. This is very important when we consider that Warriors in battle are expected to kill. That doesn't just happen. It requires the attainment of a certain state of mind and being. The purpose of war rites is to transition into and out of this state of mind so that the Warrior can function effectively in battle and then return to being a normal member of society during the peace that follows. In short, war is a transformation for the individual as well as society. The Warrior must transform themselves into the sacred state of fighting mode and then back to the holy state of peace again. War is itself an identity crisis and a transformation.

King Duncan seems oblivious to these considerations, and that is why we may infer from the story that he is not himself a Warrior, because he would otherwise have some appreciation for the dangerous period of time that follows battle. He does not allow Macbeth even a moment's rest. His announcement that he will spend the night sends his general rushing back home so that he may make arrangements for the visit. Macbeth has not had any chance to relax and reflect on the monumental events that have just occurred. He may be an experienced Warrior, but that does not mean his adrenaline is not still running high and that the other emotions that follow battle are not present. In fact, we may very well say that those emotions have attached themselves to the witches' prophecy and are driving his mind towards the idea of one more killing. A big part of the Warrior's transition into battle mode is to harden themselves against killing. An equally big part of transitioning back to peace mode is to soften oneself again. Macbeth has not made the transition back. He is still in sacred state from the battle, still in the frame of mind where killing does not have the repulsion that it should.

In themselves, these factors may not seem to amount to much, but as he always does, Shakespeare layers them on top of each other to create for the hero a unique challenge. Macbeth has the adrenaline of battle still in him. He has the knowledge that he is the greatest Warrior in the kingdom. He knows that he has just saved the kingdom from certain defeat while Duncan watched on helplessly. The witches' prophecy is now ringing in his ears, and the first part of it has seemed to come true, meaning that he can reckon with the idea of becoming king one day. On top of all this comes the final, and perhaps most important, consideration for Macbeth: his wife.

No doubt, one of the most important ways in which a Warrior transitions out of the sacred state of battle and back into the holy state of peace is the return to the family home. We have all seen images of soldiers in uniform hugging and kissing their loved ones as they return from conflict. Especially in ages where the Warrior class was not a professional one working for pay, the defence of the family home against the enemy would certainly be at the top of the list of reasons why the Warrior fights in the first place. The love and affection of the home are, at least in ideal circumstances, the opposite of the blood and death of the battlefield. The return to domestic life is therefore arguably synonymous with the re-attainment of holy state that must complete the transformation of war.

Duncan has already spoiled Macbeth's transition back to domestic life by deciding to visit his home the very same evening of the battle, thereby not allowing him to relax and readjust. But it is the attitude of Lady Macbeth herself which is the most important factor in the events which follow, and here we see another crucial implication that Shakespeare places in the story which sheds light on the kind of relationship that exists between the husband and wife. Macbeth had eagerly written to his wife telling her of the witches' prophecy and the fact that the first part of it had already come true. That shows that their relationship is very close. More specifically, it is an esoteric relationship where intimate details are shared. We must remember that this was not necessarily normal at a time when marriage among the aristocracy was businesslike (exoteric) in nature. The marriage between the Macbeths is not like that. The first thing Macbeth did on hearing the prophecy was write about it to his wife. We can infer that this is not the first time that Lady Macbeth has spurred her husband's ambitions. Perhaps she is the driving force behind his worldly success and his excellence in battle.

In this respect, the fact that the Macbeths do not have children takes on a new importance. If they did, it would be up to Lady Macbeth to take care of them, in accordance with the mores of the time. That would be especially true if there were babies and infants that needed her attention. If that were the case, then it's very likely that Lady Macbeth would not have the time or inclination to wait on letters from her husband and to give him counsel on how to respond. More broadly, what this shows is that there is already a strange and potentially dangerous conflation between Macbeth's familial and Warrior identities. Even before Duncan has stoked the flames, something is out of kilter in the Macbeth household. The implication is that Macbeth's home has not been a place of familial love prior to the events of the story. When Macbeth returns from battle, he is not greeted by a wife who is concerned to ensure he eases back into domestic life but one who is clearly excited by the opportunity that has arisen with the impending visit of Duncan.

We can see, then, that Macbeth faces a multi-faceted and multi-layered identity crisis that is as complex as Shakespeare's other great heroes. In archetypal terms, the sacrifice required is his identity as a Warrior triggering a transformation into Ruler. However, he has no legitimate right to that transformation. There is no proper exoteric pathway available to him to become Ruler. That is why he must pursue an esoteric one. As with all of Shakespeare's heroes, he must undergo a split between his exoteric and esoteric identity. In this case, the split is also one that will affect the whole kingdom, which will need to transition from the just rule of Duncan, who knows how to govern by creating a meritocracy that rewards the virtuous, to the bloody rule by the sword that Macbeth will engender when he takes the crown by force. Macbeth will never esoterically transition to the Ruler. He can only govern according to the ethos of the Warrior.

As always in Shakespeare, what sets the story apart is the degree to which the hero is conscious of the crisis he is confronting. That is unusual. Most people, when confronted with problems of any magnitude, tend to revert to subconscious behaviour. It is a natural facet of human nature to revert to the instinctual and unconscious aspects of the psyche when the pressure is on. That is not true for Shakespeare's heroes. Their purity of consciousness is all the more impressive because of the magnitude of the identity crises that they confront. Romeo and Juliet are perfectly clear and sincere in their willingness to die for love. Once we understand Hamlet's goals, we can see that he also operates with incredible clarity, all while presenting the outward appearance of the opposite. And what sets Macbeth apart is that he knows full well the gravity of what he is thinking about doing. His torturous grappling with his conscience proves that. More importantly, it shows that his journey into the sacred is self-authored. That is what differentiates Shakespeare's Adult heroes from the Orphans. The Orphans are thrown into an identity crisis they did not expect. The Adults create their own. We can tease out these details by comparing the stories of Hamlet and Macbeth.

To start with, both men are confronted with the prospect of killing a king. Hamlet has cause to do so in both a personal and political sense. That is why so many commentators have criticised him for not doing what they see as necessary and just. Apart from all the specifics that we have already gone over, it is clear that Hamlet is not an experienced Warrior and the killing of Claudius would be his first experience of such a grave act. The Warrior is dangerous precisely because they are experienced in killing, and it must be relatively easy for them, even on solely practical grounds, to kill their fellow citizens and even their leaders. The same is not true for those who have never carried out such a fateful deed. Hamlet's reluctance is perfectly understandable in this respect. Becoming a killer, even a virtuous and just one, is a major transformation in itself, one that societies construct elaborate and intricate processes around in order to safeguard the individual and the rest of society. Macbeth has already undergone that transition. Hamlet has not.

Another major difference between Hamlet's choice and Macbeth's is the question of time. Hamlet's father has been dead two months when the ghost appears. The ghost gives no specific instructions about taking revenge, including nothing about how and when it should be done. He leaves it up to Hamlet to decide. The time when quick and instant justice could have been served is gone and will never return. That is certainly one of the reasons why the prince takes the route of trying to gather evidence for Claudius' guilt. A self-confession on the part of his uncle would allow justice to occur. Failing that, and failing any other evidence that proves guilt, Hamlet can only kill without exoteric justification. As a result, the death would almost certainly not end the matter but open up all kinds of new problems. The killing can almost certainly not lead back to holy state because it is not that it is unjust; it's that it cannot be seen to be just, and in matters of politics that is a crucial factor that cannot be left out of consideration. The problem confronting Hamlet is open-ended with no obvious way to bring it to a head.

Macbeth's choice is very different because he has been gifted a golden opportunity with a very specific timeframe. Duncan will stay the night at Macbeth's estate and then leave in the morning. This is presumably a rare event. Therefore, Macbeth has one and only one chance to do the fateful deed. He does not have the luxury of time. As for questions of justice and morality, the magnitude of the decision that faces him is so great precisely because what he will be murdering with the king is not just the man but the entire idea of a society predicated on something more than brute force alone. Macbeth's internal battle against his conscience mirrors the political issue. The king is a king to the extent that he stands for what is right and just. Wars fought against enemies are not just fought for raw survival; they are fought because the Warrior believes in the righteousness of the cause. Macbeth chose to fight on the side of Duncan against the Norwegians. He must have done so because he believed in the righteousness of the cause. Otherwise, he could have easily partnered with the other rebel Thanes. Now, he is considering killing that which he believed to be right and just. By contrast, Hamlet is called on to kill a man he knows to be unjust and not righteous. But the prince knows that two wrongs do not make a right, and the only way back to holy state is via truth and justice.

Macbeth is not going to kill Duncan because he thinks the king is immoral or unjust, as Claudius is. On the contrary, Duncan is a good king, and Macbeth has just willingly fought on his side. Therefore, Macbeth is killing entirely out of ambition, and that is why he knows unequivocally that the deed cannot be justified on moral grounds. The battle that goes on within Macbeth is ambition and will against morality and justice, but that is exactly the battle between the Warrior and the Ruler. Ambition towards the goal and the willpower to achieve it are two of the primary virtues of the Warrior. When the Warrior kills the Ruler, he is elevating ambition and will over morality and justice. He creates a kingdom that can thereafter only be held together by the suppression of ambition and will in others, including those, like Banquo, who have learned to subordinate these traits to morality and justice.

Macbeth does eventually end up taking on the exoteric identity of Ruler, but esoterically, he is still a Warrior. What we see is that the qualities which are virtues in a Warrior are vices in a Ruler. A Warrior must learn to take every opportunity that is available to him to kill the enemy, and he must do so as soon as possible. The fighter who does not do this will soon be killed by the enemy who does. The Warrior archetype represents the highest exercise of the faculty of will. In the broadest terms, the Warrior must learn to attain goals. That is true of the frontline soldier on the battlefield all the way up to the highest general overseeing wars of epic proportion. But the goals are not defined by the Warrior, they are defined by the Ruler. The Ruler says when it is time to go to war. The Warrior is responsible for the conduct of the war. When ambition and will break their bounds and turn on the Ruler, there is no longer anything higher to act as a check, and ambition and will consume everything in their way. Macbeth's journey into the sacred requires him to place will and ambition above all else, and therefore it is perfectly fitting that he should kill the king since there is no higher role to attain. Of course, once the king is dead, there is nothing more to strive after. Ambition finds itself at a loss, and will that cannot be pointed outwards is turned back on itself.

All Macbeth can do is attain the exoteric role of king. To transform into the king esoterically would require him to embody the core properties of that archetype, and that means justice and morality above all else. That is why Hamlet was already esoterically a Ruler even though his uncle sat on the throne. He had already attained the requisite virtues. Macbeth may sit on the throne, but he has murdered the very esoteric qualities that would enable him to be an actual Ruler. The tragedy is that Macbeth had those qualities in him in the form of his conscience, but he kills his conscience at the same time that he kills Duncan. The sacrifice that he must make to become king guarantees his downfall. That is why the story of Macbeth is the most inevitable of Shakespeare's great works. More than any other character, we know the fate that awaits him even as he completely deludes himself that he has avoided it.

This leads to the final parallel between Hamlet and Macbeth that is worthy of mentioning. We have already seen that Hamlet was sceptical of the information given to him by the ghost. Why? Because he saw that the ghost was telling him exactly what he wanted to hear, and that is something that the devil would do. Hamlet sets out to prove one way or another whether what the ghost told him was the actual truth. Macbeth is confronted with an almost identical situation. It's not a ghost at midnight; it's three old hags in a misty forest. But the meaning is the same. The three witches tell Macbeth exactly what he wants to hear. How does Macbeth respond? He shows none of the caution and strength of mind of Hamlet. In fact, his mind is the whole problem. He can't stop thinking about the idea that the witches have planted. It's like a worm eating away at his brain.

That is another difference between the Warrior and the Ruler. A Ruler must be a sceptic because he is surrounded by people who tell him what he wants to hear in order to get what they want. A Ruler cannot trust allies any more than enemies. Both groups have a vested interest in lying to him. Moreover, even if a Ruler can get hold of quality information about how things really are, he still faces inherently complex situations full of risk and uncertainty. He must make decisions even where he cannot know the outcome. All of this requires incredible strength of mind, such as that shown by Hamlet.

By contrast, a Warrior is given a goal, a target, and an enemy. The Warrior's job is to train so that the skills to defeat the enemy become unconscious and automatic. The Warrior is much like the sportsman in that he succeeds to the extent that everything he does is turned into reflex and instinct. In that way, he can kill the enemy before he gets killed. All of this requires incredible willpower, focus, and courage. But the physical courage of the Warrior does not necessarily translate into the mental power of the Ruler. Macbeth does not have the strength of mind that Hamlet does. In fact, it would be true to say that he suffers from his own mind, and his desire to act may even be a way to try and find a release from thought. More generally, we might even say that Macbeth suffers from peace. He is the Warrior who cannot abide the holy state of intellect and wisdom but is always searching for the next enemy to conquer. When he finds none outside the kingdom, he starts looking within.

Whether that is true in general about Macbeth, it absolutely becomes true once he commits murder. When he sacrifices his conscience and king, he relinquishes the entire notion of peace resting in authority, wisdom, morality, justice, and other abstract concepts. What follows thereafter is a state of permanent war mirrored in Macbeth's own mind and the society over which he now governs. It is an irony, then, that when his confidence starts to wane, he once again returns to the witches to tell him the "truth". Macbeth still needs somebody external to guide him. He is still taking orders, only it is no longer a wise king who is giving them but three old hags. He believes them unequivocally. Now in possession of what he thinks is absolute truth, Macbeth ploughs onwards toward his doom and thinks himself invincible even when everything is stacked against him. When the reality finally reveals itself to him, we see one of the great laments in all literature: "Life's but a walking shadow...tis a tale told by an idiot, full of sound and fury, signifying nothing."

It is curious that King Lear is seen as Shakespeare's most nihilistic work. In fact, Macbeth, in the bitterness of his defeat, is Shakespeare's primary portrayal of nihilism. But it is not any statement about ultimate metaphysical reality, it is how the world appears to a man who has created a society that operates only according to violence. Having killed the source of truth and authority, Macbeth thereafter believes that there is no truth. His nihilism is entirely of his own making.

***

The inevitability of the story as it unfolds from the time when Macbeth kills Duncan has the effect of hiding what is perhaps the most profound theme that Shakespeare explores with the play. Ever since Plato's time, it has been assumed that the Warrior overthrows the Ruler because he wants power and all the things that come with it, such as wealth and fame. This foregrounds the exoteric properties of the Ruler and makes the temptation of the Warrior easy to understand from an everyday standpoint. Wealth, power, and fame are the externally visible manifestations of the archetype and are therefore easily understandable, especially since most people think their lives would be improved by the attainment of these qualities. Far fewer people understand the esoteric qualities of the Ruler among which we have listed wisdom, foresight, strength of mind, a commitment to justice, etc.

In relation to Macbeth, we have assumed that his usurpation of the throne is motivated by the traditional desires for the exoteric qualities of the Ruler. Actually, there is no evidence for that in the story. On the contrary, Macbeth is not a greedy or vainglorious man. It is not made clear whether he is striving after the exoteric or the esoteric qualities of the Ruler. We should at least entertain the hypothesis that what he really wants are the esoteric qualities of wisdom, foresight, and empathy.

This may sound outrageous. How can we possibly say that Macbeth is striving after virtue by murdering the king in his own bed without any provocation or reason? But we must not confuse the method with the goal. It is self-evident that Macbeth's actions lead him to destruction and certainly not to anything resembling wisdom or justice. However, we must remember that prior to the murder, Macbeth had an extended battle with his conscience, and what is conscience if not some combination of wisdom, foresight, and empathy? Macbeth lacks all of these later in the story, but he has them at the start. In that respect, his wrestling with his conscience is not that different from Hamlet's and the main difference between them might be that Macbeth wants the throne while Hamlet is unsure.

But even that is not the right way to put it. Hamlet already has the esoteric qualities of the Ruler. Macbeth thinks he does not. Macbeth doesn't realise that his conscience is the proof that he is already most of the way there from an esoteric point of view. His error is to think that he lacks those qualities which he already has and that the only way to attain them is to acquire the exoteric role that corresponds to them.

This raises a question that has been around since ancient times: how does one attain the esoteric qualities of a Ruler? Plato believed they had to be instilled via education. But Hamlet develops his esoteric qualities not at university but while he is away from it, and the prince clearly does not believe that philosophy holds the secret as we see in his attitude to Polonius. We might say that Hamlet inherited his virtues from his father, thereby positing a genetic cause. But if virtue runs in the family, why does his uncle Claudius have none? As we have already noted, this theme of determinism vs free will is present in all of Shakespeare's works, and he never provides any definitive answer to it. Therefore, the question remains, if Macbeth were to come to us and ask how he can attain wisdom, foresight, and empathy, what can we tell him? Should we tell him to practice philosophy as Plato does?

It is clear that the path that Macbeth chooses leads to failure. But let's think more closely about the nature of the failure. What differentiates Macbeth from the armchair philosophers who have traditionally concerned themselves with abstract concepts like wisdom and justice is that Macbeth has a real decision in front of him. His battle with his conscience is not an academic exercise but a choice to make in the real world - should he kill Duncan and take the throne? This choice is made possible because all the barriers that normally stand in the way of it have been removed. Society places significant barriers around its rulers for this exact scenario. A king is not free to walk among the people because the king is a danger to his people and they are a danger to him. For Macbeth, all of these exoteric regulations and restrictions have been removed. What's more, Macbeth is a skilled killer who has just returned from practising his trade on the battlefield. The normal psychological and practical barriers around murder have also been removed for him. Finally, it is night time, and nobody is around to see what happens. There is nothing standing between Macbeth and the object of his desire except his own conscience.

Society encourages us to be "moral" by setting up all kinds of exoteric restrictions and encouragements that make the "correct" behaviour the path of least resistance. That makes perfect sense, but the result is that most of our behaviour is being guided for us. Most things in life are therefore not a matter of conscience for us. We are not called on to make an esoteric, personal judgement, we are guided by exoteric, social norms. Therefore, most people are simply never called on to answer only to their own conscience before choosing a course of action. To do so implies the ultimate responsibility. That is the situation that Macbeth finds himself in, and that is why Macbeth can have nobody else to blame but himself.

Macbeth's dilemma is that there is something that he really wants, something of great value, and it is right there for the taking. We must remember, the desire to be king is not, in itself, wrong. Nobody would admonish a young boy for such a desire, and even in a grown man it would not be thought immoral. To allow oneself these kinds of desires is never a problem because the individual has no chance of attaining it anyway. In that case, we call it a "dream", and such dreams are harmless. What happens when the dream becomes a possibility? What happens when the opportunity is right there in front of you? We'd like to think that we would obviously grasp it with both hands, but that is almost certainly not the case because most people are simply not used to getting something of genuine value and, in a surprising number of cases, are not happy when they do (as when somebody gets rich by luck).

What lies before Macbeth is not just the question of becoming king but the broader question of creating his own identity based on inner desire and the actions required to attain it. Until now, he has been only a faithful servant, fighting whoever his king told him was the enemy. He has the opportunity to become the boss, and it is somewhat fitting that his pathway to doing so requires that he relinquish all moral restrictions on himself. What he is toying with is the ability to simply take whatever he wants in the world and allow himself no restriction on his desire. It is only his conscience that stands in the way, not the intellect or abstract reasoning of the armchair philosopher.

Let's imagine that Macbeth had chosen differently. Let's imagine that he steals into Duncan's bedroom, holds the knife to his throat, and only at the last second withdraws. In that case, Macbeth would have made a commitment to morality and justice that is stronger than any philosophical treatise. It would not be based in reason and logic but in lived experience. More importantly, it would not be based on the social conventions and other exoteric guardrails that society constructs. It would be entirely esoteric in nature.

But that is already the exact battle that Macbeth goes through. That is what the story of Macbeth is about. He is already one step away from killing Duncan. There is nothing practically in his way. He makes his decision, but we can easily imagine the decision going the other way, and if it did, we would have to say that Macbeth has more moral integrity than any philosopher or priest because he stood on the precipice and did not fall.

There is a certain irony to all this because it's the philosophers and armchair critics who all chastise Hamlet for not simply killing his uncle Claudius as if it were the easiest thing in the world to do. How many of those critics had ever served in the military? How many of them had ever killed somebody? The answer is almost certainly none. They were not speaking from lived experience but from academic considerations.

Macbeth is the complement to Hamlet. He is the man who really does thrust the blade in and suffer the consequences. Macbeth comes to learn directly why justice and morality exist and why the authority of the king should be respected even if we don't rationally understand why. That's why it is fitting that Macbeth's downfall comes even while he believes that he holds an eternal truth in his mind that will protect him from the consequences of his actions.

This is another way in which he is highly prophetic of the 20th century. So much of the bloodshed at that time came from people who firmly believed the truths they possessed were greater than morality and justice. They had convinced themselves that duties to moral precepts were held together by nothing more than blind obedience to authority. They believed that their intellectual theories would bind everything together on the other side of the destruction of authority. In the end, they learned the same lesson as Macbeth: that what is born out of violence and murder can only be held together by the same methods. In such cases, a blind obedience to authority is replaced by an equally blind belief in intellectual truths.

What we see in Macbeth is one of the fundamental issues that is explored in all Shakespeare's works. The only way we can esoterically grasp the exoteric bonds that bind us is by challenging them. The challenge to this authority is perhaps the most dangerous journey into the sacred that exists because the bonds may easily break and then we are left naked. When we call into question that which is most holy, we open ourselves to that which is most sacred. Hamlet is thrust into the challenge unexpectedly. Macbeth chooses it freely. It is the latter who ends up in nihilism and despair, and that is one more reason why Macbeth is highly prophetic of our time.

Othello

Every story is about the transformation of the hero. That has been our mantra, and, up until now, there has been no ambiguity about who the actual hero of the story is, notwithstanding that all characters have their own transformation to navigate. In most of Shakespeare's works, it's possible to know the hero from the title alone – King Lear, Macbeth, Romeo and Juliet, Richard III, Henry IV; the list goes on. But as the Bard is wont to do, he breaks the rules every now and again to keep us on our toes. The convention that the title of the work should denote the hero is one such rule, and there are at least two plays where Shakespeare breaks it. The first is Julius Caesar, where the hero of the story is not Casesar but Brutus. The second is the work to which we now turn. Othello is not the hero of the story. That role goes to the man who destroys him, Iago.

This assertion gives us occasion to consider in more detail the nature of Shakespeare's heroes and how we may identify them with a degree of certainty. What distinguishes them first and foremost is their clarity of consciousness about the sacrifice they make at the beginning of their journey. Macbeth is the prime example here. His wrestling with his conscience prior to the fateful murder of Duncan shows that he understands the gravity of the situation. The same is true of Romeo and Juliet. Even in the passion of young love, they nevertheless know the stakes they face. They also know with certainty that they would rather kill themselves than be separated from each other. That is the sacrifice they are willing to make. We could expand this list of examples to all the works of Shakespeare.

We must be clear; the consciousness of the hero does not guarantee success because any journey into the sacred is necessarily filled with risk and ambiguity. Shakespeare's heroes understand that too. Their consciousness is not just intelligence or wisdom; it is something deeper. It is a leap into the unknown driven by some fundamental will or resolve. For this reason, we may say that all of Shakespeare's heroes are attempting to create their own destiny in the face of obstacles which others would consider insurmountable. This brings to mind the concept of hubris that we introduced earlier in the book. But it is precisely the brightness of their consciousness that saves them from hubris because we normally associate hubris with somebody who is ignorant of the potential consequences of their actions but who ploughs on anyway and, when they are brought undone, are none the wiser. By contrast, Shakespeare's heroes are not only fully aware of what they are getting themselves into; they are fully aware when it all goes wrong. They have the courage and strength of character to face up to the bitter truth without dissembling. It is this which redeems them, even when they end up as horrid villains like Macbeth.

If clarity of consciousness is the primary quality of the Shakespearean hero, we can see the problem raised earlier in the book about Hamlet and King Lear. Commentators have struggled to understand the actions of these two heroes and have sought to explain them away by vague concepts like Lear being "mad" or Hamlet being "melancholy". But that simply will not do. Shakespeare's heroes always have clarity about what they are doing. If we do not understand them, then the fault is ours, and we must redouble our efforts.

If we apply this criterion of clarity to the story of Othello, we can see that the titular hero does not act with the level of conscious understanding that we expect of a Shakespearean hero. On the contrary, Othello belongs to another kind of character who appears in all of the Bard's works, the ones who are good-natured but easily deceived. King Duncan is a prime example; arguably, Lord and Lady Capulet are too. Hero and Claudio in Much Ado About Nothing and Gloucester in King Lear are other exemplars. These individuals have their own journey into the sacred to go through, and they do have the strength of character to face up to the truth when it is revealed. However, they are not the heroes because they are not the instigators of the transformation.

The Shakespearean hero is the one who sets events in motion and is fully conscious of the fact that they are doing so.

One of the things that makes Othello so fascinating as a story is that the Moorish general has indeed made a sacrifice in the beginning by secretly marrying a woman who is forbidden to him by the conventions of the society in which he resides but is not a citizen. Othello is certainly conscious of the difficulties this raises, and in that respect we would say he is a Shakespearean hero as far as that side of the story goes. However, the story that we see unfold before us is not driven by Othello but by the man who realises he can manipulate Othello's journey into the sacred. In a sense, Iago hijacks Othello's story. Because he does so via subterfuge, Othello is not conscious of what is happening and doesn't learn the truth until it is too late. Iago is the one who has full consciousness of what is occurring. Therefore, Iago is the real hero of the story.

Now that we know who the hero is, our next task is the familiar one of tracing back to the holy state that exists prior to the start of the journey. As usual, the holy state is communicated to us via Shakespeare's favourite method of covert exposition. Othello contains a complex backstory that requires us to understand both the holy state of the general and of Iago. Let's begin with the Moor.

In Othello, we have a character similar to Macbeth. He is an older Warrior in the prime of his life. Unlike Macbeth, who is a cousin to the king who is defending his homeland from foreign invasion, Othello is a mercenary fighter who sells his services to the leaders of Venice. As a result, he is not a citizen, and it is made clear that the privileges he enjoys are predicated on his performance on the battlefield. Othello seems perfectly happy with this arrangement and knows his own value. That is the holy state that he is in before the action begins. He has a stable identity that he is comfortable with.

The break in the holy state begins in the weeks and months prior to the beginning of the action. A wealthy Venetian called Brabantino has taken a liking to the general and invites him to his home regularly so that Othello may regale him with stories of his great deeds in battle. However, there is another member of Brabantino's household who also takes a liking to the Moor, and that is his unmarried daughter, Desdemona. We learn that Desdemona has knocked back numerous suitors from the best families in Venice. Until now, she has proven herself uninterested in marriage, but she falls for Othello, and he reciprocates.

The great Warrior has found love, and love in Shakespeare always ends in marriage. Therein lies the problem because Othello's special status as a mercenary fighter, not to mention his skin colour, means he is a questionable match for Desdemona. The two lovers find themselves in an identical position to Romeo and Juliet. They pursue the exact same strategy of marrying in secret rather than getting paternal approval first. Their plan is to get married and then present it as a *fait accompli* to Brabantino. Since he clearly likes Othello, this strategy has a good chance of working but is not without risk. All of this is indicative of the sacred state of a love story, which is exactly what has taken place between Othello and Desdemona prior to the opening of the play.

The happy couple's journey into the sacred should be coming to an end. They have been married but have not yet broken the news to Brabantino. That is the situation when the play begins, and that is where Iago comes into the picture. To understand his position, let's also sketch out his holy state via the covert exposition that Shakespeare gives us.

The holy state for Iago also takes place several weeks prior to the beginning of the action. As a professional soldier, he belongs to the Warrior archetype. However, we would not say that Iago manifests the highest virtues of the Warrior. For him, war is a job, one that he conducts with the same degree of dispassion as the rest of his life. There is no ambiguity about this; it is what Iago tells Roderigo in the opening scene:-

You shall mark many a duteous and knee-crooking knave,
That doting on his own obsequious bondage wears out his time,
Much like his master's ass, for nought but provender,
And when he's old, Cashier'd,
Whip me such honest knaves.
Others there are who, trimm'd in forms and visages of duty,
Keep yet their hearts attending on themselves...

Iago carries out his duties not out of any love for his homeland or respect for his superiors but out of pure self-interest. It is this same attitude that has brought him into contact with Roderigo.

Iago makes a bit of cash on the side by engaging in what we would nowadays call con jobs, i.e., he gains the trust of the mark and strings them along while extracting money or other resources from them. Roderigo is a wealthy Venetian who is infatuated with Desdemona. Iago has promised to bring them together, something which he can do because his wife, Emilia, is Desdemona's maidservant. However, we can see from the opening interaction with Brabantino that Desdemona has already rejected Roderigo's advances. Since Iago has already extracted whatever money he can get, this would normally be the time when he severs ties with Roderigo and moves on to find the next sucker.

Thus, the holy state for Iago is that he is a married man with a stable job as a soldier and a side business that is immoral, if not illegal, but presumably earns him some useful pocket money. That is the exoteric side of his identity. The esoteric is also clear. Iago is a cynic who claims to believe in reason. His ability to use his intellect to fool others gives him great satisfaction. Once again, we don't need to speculate on this. He tells us himself in the soliloquy that ends Act 1:

Thus do I ever make my fool my purse;
For I mine own gain'd knowledge should profane,
If I would time expend with such a snipe but for my sport and profit.

Sport and profit have been Iago's primary motives up until now. These belong to the holy state of the conman, the world that he knows and is comfortable in.

But in the very same soliloquy that ends the first act of the play, we see what signifies Iago's own transition out of holy state and into sacred state. The opening scene shows us that Roderigo is incensed that Iago was promising him access to Desdemona at the same time that he knew that she had been planning marriage with Othello. In short, Roderigo has begun to realise that he has been conned. That is one problem for Iago.

The more important problem is that he had recently sought a promotion to lieutenant, even organising three dignitaries to plead on his behalf. But Othello awarded the job to Cassio instead. In the weeks leading up to the start of the story, Othello has cost Iago twice, once in his official profession and once in his secretive con work. That forms the basis of his resentment towards the Moor.

Thus, the meeting in the opening scene of the play between Iago and Roderigo, which just happens to take place right near the house of Brabantino, is no accident. Iago has set things up to get revenge on Othello. He has Roderigo alert Brabantino about the secret marriage of his daughter, something that Iago has inside knowledge about through his wife. That not only spoils Othello's plan of breaking the news to Desdemona's father privately, it actually threatens to have the Moor thrown in jail after Brabantino forms a mob to arrest him. If this trick had been successful, it would have solved Iago's problem by getting Roderigo off his back. But the plan fails, and Iago doubles down.

Setting aside the details, what is crucial about this is that Iago is no longer operating according to his maxim of "sport and profit". Something more personal is going on. One of the reasons this represents Iago's transition out of holy state and into sacred state is because it violates his own stated principle of not allowing the baser instincts to triumph over reason. This is how he explains it to Roderigo:-

> *If the balance of our lives had not one scale of reason to poise another of sensuality, the blood and baseness of our natures would conduct us to the most preposterous conclusions: but we have reason to cool our raging motions, our carnal stings, our unbitted lusts; whereof I will take this, that you call love, to be a sect or scion.*

Part of what makes Iago a complex and interesting character is that there is a philosophy behind his actions. When we say that he is a cynic, that is not simply meant in the modern sense of his having a distrustful and pessimistic nature, although Iago certainly has that. Rather, Iago is a cynic in the sense of the ancient philosophical sect which, among other things, rejected social conventions and romantic love. On the question of love, Iago's mockery of Roderigo is genuine, and his later attempt to destroy the love of Othello and Desdemona is fully in line with his philosophy on life, that of the cynic. (For this reason, the character of Iago is perhaps Shakespeare's most brutal attack on philosophy).

Iago's cynicism is tied in with his view on life that reason should keep the base emotions in check. That is why the opening scene represents his transition into sacred state because Iago is no longer acting according to reason and business. He has allowed the baseness of his own nature to start to operate. Resentment, bitterness, and hate have begun to drive his actions. We can see that by the fact that he believes an absurd rumour that Othello has slept with his own wife. At exactly the time that he is warning Roderigo away from "preposterous conclusions", Iago has started to believe his own.

Thus, when his first plan to ruin Othello fails because the Moor wins the support of the Senate, who want to send him to a war in Cyprus, Iago immediately conceives a much riskier con. He tells Roderigo to travel to the war with the promise of uniting him with Desdemona. That is a wild claim that he has no way of delivering on. More importantly, Iago is now mixing his official exoteric identity as a soldier with his esoteric side project as a swindler. As if that wasn't enough, Desdemona will also be in Cyprus due to the fact that her father has disowned her. That means Iago's wife will be there too since she is still employed as Desdemona's maidservant. All the aspects of Iago's identity converge in a very dangerous fashion, hence the final line of his soliloquy that ends the first act: "It is engender'd. Hell and night must bring this monstrous birth to the world's light." This is Iago's official transition into sacred state, and we can see that he makes it with the full consciousness that befits a Shakespearean hero.

However, there is a larger reason why Iago's plan is "monstrous". Up until now, Iago has been in it for "sport and profit". He enjoys being a conman for the money he receives but also for the joy that comes from proving other people stupider than himself. That makes some sense, and it's possible to imagine the thrill that comes with a job that involves removing fools from their money. But the con he has now cooked up gains Iago nothing. There is no money involved, and he is no longer tricking gullible fools like Roderigo; he is trying to break up a relationship that is clearly based in true love and affection. Iago's journey into the sacred is motivated by nothing more than resentment and bitterness, and if anything belongs to "the blood and baseness of our natures", it is that. Apart from anything else, this is a violation of his own cynic philosophy of detachment.

Thus, Iago's villainy is very different to the types we have seen thus far. Claudius and Macbeth get to become king. That is the reason for their actions. Edmund in King Lear gets to become the Earl of Gloucester. The risk that these characters take earns them something in return. There is a genuine transformation of their identity. We can criticise them on multiple fronts for their actions, but we must accept that they were pursuing some kind of positive goal. Iago will receive nothing by destroying the marriage of Othello and Desdemona. There is no new identity awaiting him on the other side of that goal, no payoff at all. Iago knows full well that what he is doing is simply to destroy for the sake of destroying. That is why his actions are monstrous.

Despite that, it is still true that Iago is making a sacrifice because he is taking a huge risk. Up until now, his con jobs have been small and self-contained in nature. What he will now set about doing is a multi-person con job that involves Roderigo, Cassio, Othello, Desdemona, and his own wife, Emilia. The complexity of it hugely increases the risk that he will get caught, and, if he gets caught, the stakes are very high indeed. It may well be that Othello kills him directly or that he receives the same penalty by the Venetian courts. Iago is staking his own life on the outside chance of getting revenge for what amounts to a minor gripe.

What we see in Iago is at once both a perfectly normal transition from holy state to sacred state and yet also something very different from anything we have encountered thus far. We have said that the holy state is about knowledge, reason, and consciousness, while the sacred state is largely the opposite of these. Iago begins as a philosopher preaching a gospel of reason. That is both his personal holy state and one that fits with the broader concept of holiness.

His transition to sacred state sees him relinquish that for the base emotions of hatred, bitterness, and resentment. To say it again, though, this willing embrace of the base emotions is not something we have seen before. Macbeth ends up adopting these attributes, but that was not his intention. He thought he could commit an evil act and then avoid the consequences. Reality showed him otherwise. With Iago, we have a man who knows that he is embracing bitterness and hatred and proceeds anyway with no other goal in mind. Even more incredible is the fact that he successfully pulls off a con job that involves an intricate and sophisticated deception over an extended period of time. It is this combination of factors that makes Iago one of the most unique characters in all literature.

We have now sketched out the two intersecting journeys into the sacred that form the core of the story. Othello and Desdemona are sacrificing their present identity for the chance of love. Iago is sacrificing his for hate. We can deepen our understanding of the dynamic by employing our archetypal lens on the characters.

Desdemona needs little further elaboration because we have seen this scenario already. As an aristocratic woman, her entry into the Adult phase of life comes with marriage, and that is exactly what has just happened. However, her marriage to Othello has forced her to sever ties with her family, and so she has lost her familial identity. This leaves her in a very precarious situation if Iago manages to pull off his con because a breakup in the marriage with Othello would leave her in limbo without a family to return to. In any case, we say that she has only just entered the Adult phase of life and has still not really completed the transition from Orphan to Adult.

As for Iago and Othello, we know that both are in the Adult phase of life with an economic identity of Warrior. The crucial difference is in their familial identity. Iago has been married for some time, and we learn later that his marriage is as loveless as his philosophy. Othello is a newlywed who is very much in love with Desdemona. Like Desdemona, he has not fully realised the transition into marriage due to Iago's actions in the opening scene. As if that wasn't enough, Othello has been instructed to fight the war against the Turks in Cyprus. He decides to take Desdemona along, meaning that their honeymoon is going to take place in a war zone, which is obviously not conducive to a return to holy state. Thus, Othello has also not yet made the proper transition from Orphan to Adult in relation to his familial identity.

In archetypal terms, Othello's position is also familiar to us by now because he is in the same situation as Don Pedro and Benedick in Much Ado About Nothing in that he is an older man with an established economic identity who has just found love. That means he is on the verge of establishing the final aspect of his mature Adult identity by starting a family of his own. It is that which Iago has set out to destroy, which means he is really destroying the Adult identity for both Othello and Desdemona. Iago is trying to ruin two lives all over a petty slight to his honour. But, to say it again, even if he succeeds, he wins nothing new in terms of his own identity. He will still be an unhappily married man with a job he cares little about.

With that, we have summarised the incredibly intricate backstory that frames the action of the play. What is left to say is something about the meaning of the overall story. Even this is a surprise and needs to be teased out via implication.

What we have are two married couples where the husbands are both Warriors. One couple is from the aristocracy, Othello and Desdemona, and the other is from the general public, Iago and Emilia. The latter pair work directly for the former, giving us a pair of master-servant relationships. The four of them all travel to what they expect to be a war zone, but they learn on arrival that the war is cancelled because the Turks have run aground and died. What will take place instead is a strange kind of domestic situation where the newlywed couple will be "advised" by the more experienced one.

At the exact same time that this theme is running, we can detect another theme by splitting the pairs by sex. What we then find is that the war metaphor is carried over into a classic battle-of-the-sexes dynamic. It turns out that the story of Othello is Shakespeare's primary meditation on married life. The bitter and cynical older couple of Iago and Emilia will provide a terrible initiation to the newlyweds Othello and Desdemona, one that destroys their marriage before it has even begun.

Just as in Much Ado About Nothing, the drama will revolve around the man's jealousy masquerading as pride and the woman's honour, which is easily smeared by nothing more than innuendo. Note that Don John's machinations in Much Ado were also a kind of con job in that he made Don Pedro and Claudio believe what was not true. Iago is a far more experienced campaigner, and his con is infinitely more sophisticated. He breaks Othello down one step at a time, simultaneously creating the illusion he wants to show and then biasing the mind of his master towards the interpretation that he desires. In that respect, Othello is also an incredible psychological and even philosophical work because it shows in real time how we can be made to read into events what is not there.

This raises similarities with Macbeth because Macbeth also learns to see in events what is only really in his mind. The difference is that Macbeth wants the witches' prophecy to be true. Othello absolutely does not want what Iago is telling him to be true, and he is not as easily swayed as the weaker minds of Don Pedro and Claudio. Neither he nor Desdemona are naturally inclined to fall into such petty traps. Both of them have too much nobility of soul for that and are too much in love. Ultimately, the best comparison here is with Romeo and Juliet. We have two lovers who are prepared to sacrifice all for each other. Yet another reason why Iago's plan is so devastating is because he is setting out to destroy the purest of love.

Although Iago is the instigator, we see that his wife Emilia ends up also becoming a cynical guide for the newly married Desdemona, and this is where the contrast between the older married couple and the younger becomes most pronounced. Emilia is also disillusioned towards the idea of love, as evidenced by the counsel she gives to Desdemona:-

> *'Tis not a year or two shows us a man:*
> *They are all but stomachs and we all but food;*
> *They eat us hungerly, and when are full*
> *They belch us.*

The tragedy for Emilia is that the disputes between her mistress and Othello are only occurring because her own husband is pulling the strings behind the scenes. Emilia is not only oblivious to that, she is an unwitting assistant. That is why she must also share in the blame because her disillusionment has meant that she no longer takes any interest in her husband and has no idea what he is up to. By being so disconnected in her own marriage, Emilia is helping to destroy another.

Thus, the difference between Iago and Emilia is that the former is acting with perfect consciousness of what he is doing and the latter is completely unconscious of the role she is playing. Her sacrifice is made by being completely ignorant of her husband. The loss of that ignorance turns to horror in the final scene as Emilia realises not just what Iago has done in relation to the destruction of Othello and Desdemona but who he has been the whole time they have been married. She comes to the realisation that she has not even known the man that was right in front of her eyes. In that respect, she is very much like other tragic characters in Shakespeare who suffer for their ignorance, Gloucester in King Lear being a prime example.

The battle-of-the-sexes dynamic plays out alongside everything else that is going on. We have had several occasions to touch on the patriarchal world in which Shakespeare's stories take place. Iago and Othello have what we now call day jobs, and, in fact, they are technically at work throughout the story since, although the war has not come to pass, they are still under orders from Venice, and that comes with various tasks to be done. In that respect, Desdemona's lobbying on behalf of the innocent Cassio is actually a kind of meddling in Othello's occupation, something that he never had to deal with before as a single man. Meanwhile, Othello's increasingly poisonous mood can also be thought of metaphorically as him "bringing home his work" since it is his subordinate Iago who is the cause of the trouble.

Indeed, Othello is perhaps the most metaphorical of all Shakespeare's works. Where does this domestic episode take place? In the warzone of Cyprus. Othello and Desdemona are trying to learn the roles of husband and wife while in the middle of a war. For Iago and Emilia, marriage is already war, where the enemy is one's spouse who is to be defeated using whatever weapons will get the job done. That is the lesson they attempt to pass on to Othello and Desdemona. Thus it is that Desdemona, following the argument with Othello that occurs in Act 3, Scene 4, refers to herself as an "unhandsome warrior" (meaning an inadequate or incompetent fighter). It is the first "fight" between the newlyweds, and she has no idea how to proceed. Desdemona can be forgiven her ignorance, just like Othello can be forgiven his. But who is guiding Desdemona? The bitter and cynical Emilia. And who is guiding Othello? The even more bitter and resentful Iago. Their initiation into marriage is doomed from the start.

Falling in love is one thing. Being married is something else. In Shakespeare, the former belongs to the Orphan phase of life and the latter to the Adult phase. A transition is needed between the two, and that is what Othello and Desdemona are going through. Just like politics, marriage entails conflict, and conflict must be resolved. Warriors like Iago and Othello attempt to resolve that conflict using their own weapons. Thus, it is fitting that both men draw their swords on Emilia in the final scene of the play. When threatened with physical violence, she retorts, "I care not for thy sword, I'll make thee known." Women's weapons are words. Emilia uses her voice to bring both men undone.

If we set aside the specific details, what is going on in Othello at the more abstract level is the first argument between a husband and wife. That argument revolves around perhaps the oldest and most universal conflict, a story that can be found in every culture: the perceived coquettishness of the woman and the subsequent jealousy in the man. Neither of these behaviours has an objective standard that can determine the "truth". There is an inevitable and substantial grey area that, if left unresolved, leads to the mutual incomprehension that the long-married couple like Emilia and Iago demonstrate. Emilia and Iago have never resolved their conflicts and therefore they don't understand each other at all. Their entire marriage is one long battle without end. Desdemona does not know what to do because she has never been around men. Othello does not yet understand female behaviour because he has spent his whole life among men fighting in battle. Their only guides are a cynical older couple. All of this is the inversion of the dynamic from Much Ado About Nothing. In that story, it was the older couple, Beatrice and Benedick, who helped to save the younger one from the exact same problem of jealousy and an attack on the woman's honour. They did that because they still believed in love. Iago and Emilia no longer believe in love, and perhaps never did.

But, actually, that is not entirely correct, and here we come to the crux of the story. Iago does not believe in love. That much is crystal clear. But Emilia still does. We have spoken several times now about the role of the witness as the one who transmits the truth at the end of a Shakespearean story. Emilia will become the witness, and she is the most impassioned witness we have seen so far. She is the one who discovers that Othello has killed Desdemona and then realises that it is her own husband who has been pulling the strings from behind the scenes, including his manipulation of her throughout their marriage. Emilia has learned cynicism from her husband, but her vehement outburst in the final scene proves that she still knows the difference between love, truth and beauty and their opposites.

Emilia becomes a witness to the two intersecting journeys into the sacred that form the basis of the play. The first of these is the love story between Othello and Desdemona, which ends in tragedy. It is crucial that we understand the nature of that tragedy because it determines our understanding of the resolution of the second journey into the sacred, which is that of Iago. To proceed, we must bring to mind once again our distinction between the exoteric and esoteric as it specifically relates to the question of honour and pride, the external and internal manifestations of identity respectively. Because we don't understand the concept of honour anymore in modern Western society, we believe that Othello kills Desdemona out of jealousy alone. In other words, we believe his motivations are entirely esoteric in nature. In fact, that is not the case and the story makes this very clear.

Othello is a Warrior and a general. Honour is of the highest importance in the world in which he lives. That is why Cassio is so mortified when Iago tricks him into despoiling his own honour. It is why Iago is able to get away with his deception because, in his own words, he is "trimm'd in forms and visages of duty". He knows how to maintain his honour and project an image of himself as a faithful servant. The world in which the story of Othello takes place is first and foremost concerned with outward appearances. Honour must be upheld at all costs, and it is the responsibility of the individual to protect their honour.

It is precisely because Iago knows how to maintain exoteric appearances that he is able to operate so effectively as a conman. By contrast, Othello does not know how to operate in the esoteric domain, and that is why Iago is able to fool him. But we must be absolutely clear that, although jealously plays a role, Othello's main concern in relation to Desdemona is the question of honour. If his new wife has ruined her honour via a dalliance with Cassio, that is the end of their marriage because the concept of love as they understand it includes notions of duty which are exoteric in nature.

It is this which leads to the final devastating scene which many of us in the modern world must struggle to understand because we don't know about honour. Othello still (esoterically) loves Desdemona even as he kills her. Desdemona still loves Othello even though she knows she must die. That is why, when Desdemona answers Emilia's question over who killed her, her response that she killed herself is metaphorically true. Desdemona must have known the risks she was taking with her honour when she secretly married Othello. For a woman in her era, honour was a basic fact of life, not a moral issue to be speculated upon. Just like Hero in Much Ado About Nothing, this leaves Desdemona powerless but not ignorant. Her situation is not a moral one; it is a factual one. Her honour has been compromised. Therefore, she is ruined.

It is because the issue at hand is primarily honour that Othello can truthfully state to Lodovico after the killing of Desdemona that he is "an honourable murderer, if you will; for nought did I in hate, but all in honour." As hard as it is for us to imagine, Othello still loves the woman he murders. Therefore, what we see in the final scene between the two lovers is something very similar to Romeo and Juliet. It is about the consequences of the failure to unite their exoteric and esoteric identities. Othello and Desdemona die as Romeo and Juliet do, still in love in the esoteric sense.

Once we understand this, we also understand the resolution to Iago's journey. Iago is the only one who does not believe in love. Iago is the only one who has actual hate inside him. Othello speaks truly when he says, "For nought did I in hate". Thus, although Iago's plan has "worked" in the exoteric sense, one thing he has not managed to do is instil his own jealousy, hatred, and nihilism into the heart of his master. That is also true of Desdemona, who never takes seriously the cynical advice of Emilia. Despite all of the exoteric circumstances being against her, Desdemona love remains esoterically true. Despite Iago's incredible campaign of psychological manipulation, Othello never learns to hate. Thus, Iago achieves his goal in the exoteric domain only. In the esoteric, he may be able to temporarily bend others to his own cynical and pessimistic worldview, but they never truly become like him, not even the woman he was married to for many years.

The resolution to Iago's journey is therefore the consummation of the gamble that he took at the beginning. In order to give vent to his hatred, he needed to sacrifice his secrecy. The visage of the dutiful servant that he had managed to keep up for his whole life gets destroyed, and Iago is made to reveal to the world what he really is. The conman and deceiver is seen by others for the first time.

And this leads to the final incredible twist. We said that Iago was the hero because he is the one who consciously takes the journey into the sacred at the start of the story. But every journey into the sacred must be part of a larger transformation which either succeeds or fails. Iago's plan to ruin Othello and Desdemona has actually succeeded, and what actually happens in the final scene is that Iago's exoteric and esoteric identities become unified for the first time in his life. As counterintuitive as it may be, Iago achieves a "holy state" at the end of the story. When that normally happens, we call the story a comedy. But, even in a comedy, the hero must have changed because every story must be about transformation. However, that is not true of Iago. He has not transformed at all. He spent the entire time doing what he has always done: scamming others. The only thing that has changed is that he got caught. The paradox of the ending is that Iago achieves "holy state" by being revealed for what he is. He becomes holy at the time when his identity is destroyed.

Meanwhile, the other three characters for whom the story is a tragedy, Othello, Desdemona, and Emilia, undergo their own transformation. Their transformation is about coming to grips with the fact that there is evil in the world that will destroy what is beautiful and good for no reason. Iago is a representation of that evil which does not change or transform, it is just a background part of life. It has no logical or rational reason to exist. It just is. Thus, the final exchange between Othello and Iago is perfectly observed:-

Othello: Will you, I pray, demand that demi-devil, Why he hath thus ensnared my body and soul?

Iago: Demand me nothing; what you know, you know: From this time forth I never will speak word.

Iago gives no reason because he has no reason. He was never going to gain anything from his plan but he did it anyway. Iago begins and ends the story where Macbeth finishes – in nihilism. The world for him is nothing more than a farce, something to be manipulated for his own ends. That is how he treats his wife, his colleagues, his boss, his clients (Roderigo), and even strangers like Desdemona.

Although Iago's hatred triumphs in the sense that he achieves his mission of destroying the other characters, and although he thereby proves once again the superiority of his intellect, the one thing he fails to successfully implant in the others is his own hatred. As the above passage proves, Othello still doesn't understand at the end of the story why Iago has done what he has done. Neither do the others. They are the heroes of the story precisely because they cannot understand Iago. Emilia dies still believing in truth and love. Othello and Desdemona die still in love. They are forever superior to the cynic and the nihilist.

King Lear

Before we get into the details of King Lear, there is a point that has been implied in our analysis so far that is worth making explicit. Shakespeare's work constitutes what we might call "high art". With our modern entertainment industry and the enormous volume of content it creates, we have become accustomed to storytelling that relies on plot contrivances rather than deep insight into human nature. Most of the time, storytellers scarcely bother to have the plot contrivances remain logically consistent. Thus, there is a whole genre of satirical commentary that pokes fun at the plot holes in even some of the biggest-selling films of all time. Filmmakers and authors paper over these problems by ensuring that the pace of the plot is such that the audience does not have time to notice.

By contrast, Shakespeare's stories are much "slower" both in terms of plot and also by the fact that there is no action going on in the background as a distraction. In fact, in stage performances, the other characters barely move so that attention can be focused on the current speaker. The physical requirements of changing stage scenery also constrict the pace at which the story can proceed. All of this gives the audience time to digest what has just happened and think about what it means. The mental tempo of the whole production differs from the frantic pace of modern film.

This is made up for by the fact that every line and every action in the play is imbued with meaning. Nothing that is ever said or done in a Shakespeare story is by accident. Every phrase has weight, and our job as the audience is to grasp it. This is perhaps the primary difference between high art and pop art. In pop art, the audience is encouraged to let things slide by the pace of the production. To focus too intently would make you realise the gaping plot holes and destroy the illusion; hence the phrase "leave your brain at the door". It is this default way of interpreting art that we must overcome in respect to Shakespeare. We cannot leave our brains at the door if we want to understand King Lear. Every line has meaning. Nothing can be ignored.

But we also know by now that there is a wealth of meaning that Shakespeare communicates via his covert exposition. Not only can we not ignore what is shown to us, we must also be able to detect and decode what is being implied. What is not said is often just as important as what is. This is where our distinction between the exoteric and esoteric becomes not just a crucial fact in understanding the identities of the characters in the story but a vital technique to grasp the meaning of events. It is the failure to understand the covert exposition in the story that has led seemingly all commentators and critics to misunderstand King Lear. Thus, almost all of the analysis we are about to undertake will be dedicated to grasping the implied backstory and how it creates for Lear the challenge that he is trying to overcome when the play starts. It is time to bring out the big guns. If we are going to grasp the true meaning of Lear, we will need to draw on all the concepts that we have been utilising throughout this book. Let's begin.

***

The standard interpretation of King Lear is that it's a story about an old king who is no longer of sound mind. The play begins with a fateful decision about dividing his kingdom up, which goes wrong due to the vainglorious nature of Lear, who then loses his temper, banishing his favourite daughter, Cordelia, and his best advisor, Kent. Things go from bad to worse as the king's daughters betray him. They throw him out into a storm; he goes mad, then, after a brief reunion with Cordelia, is defeated in battle and dies.

A half-mad old man makes a stupid error, goes fully mad and then dies. Does this sound like a story worthy of Shakespeare? Recall the incredible inner struggle that Macbeth has with his conscience over a fateful deed that he has only one chance to commit. Think about the adaptiveness and ingenuity of Iago and the grand battle Othello has against the illusions of his servant. Remember the desperate attempts of Romeo and Juliet to consecrate their love and the fidelity of their commitment to die rather than sacrifice it. The standard interpretation of Lear contains none of this. There is no real struggle at all. Lear loses his mind and then everything falls apart. The end. Commentators have simply shrugged and said that it's a work of nihilism, a bleak, unremitting tale of needless, meaningless suffering.

All of this is wrong. For one thing, it violates the principle we outlined in our analysis of Othello that every Shakespearean hero has an incredible clarity of consciousness about the sacrifice they are making when the story begins and then about the consequences of that sacrifice when they are fully known at the end. Of course, we also know that Shakespeare loves to break the rules for effect, and so it may very well be that he is doing so in this case. But where, then, would be the other character in the story who may take on the role as the one who understands the sacrifice? They also don't seem to exist. Hence the themes of nihilism and despair that have been attributed to the play.

In fact, Lear is a true Shakespearean hero, probably the greatest of all. To discern the nature of the sacrifice he makes and why he makes it, we must learn to see as he does. To do that, we need to unpack the covert exposition of the story as usual. But we also need to supplement this with another activity we have engaged in throughout our analysis, and that is filling in the cultural and historical context to the story.

We already know that Elizabethan England was a patriarchy in which primogeniture was practised. Inheritance went to the eldest son on the death of the father. For royal families, the inheritance included the crown. Unlike in the Denmark of Hamlet, this was a rule that was not to be violated. Elizabethan audiences were intimately familiar with that rule because the life of their own queen, and the trajectory of their nation, had been upended by it. Henry VIII's wife, Catherine of Aragon, did not bear him a son. In order to get one, he needed to have his marriage to her annulled. When the Pope refused, Henry severed ties with Rome, created the Church of England, and married Anne Boleyn. Henry overturned the kingdom in order to get a son. Although his son Edward did become king, ironically, it was Henry's daughter Elizabeth who would reign the longest. She died just two years prior to Shakespeare writing King Lear.

This famous piece of English history has a longer but much less famous backstory. A big part of the reason why Henry VIII was so obsessed with a son was because of the memory of an earlier episode from the 12th century which has direct parallels with the story of Lear. The first (unofficial) queen of England was called Matilda. She was designated heir by her ageing father, Henry I, after the death of his son, William. When Henry died, Matilda was overseas in Normandy. Before she could travel back to be crowned, the throne was seized by her cousin Stephen. Matilda returned to fight with help from the Earl of Gloucester. There followed a long civil war called 'The Anarchy', which was a disaster for the nation. The cause of the calamity was put down to the violation of the rule of primogeniture. All of the way until Henry VIII's time, people believed that a female heir to the throne would cause an identical catastrophe.

Consider, then, that the story of Lear had been around for centuries before Shakespeare made his adaptation and that it seems to be loosely based on the events of the 12th century. There is a king with no sons and three female heirs. One of those heirs will return from France to fight a war, and one of the major characters in the story is Gloucester. It's quite likely that earlier audiences might have connected the whole thing back to the civil war and attributed the tragedy to the violation of primogeniture.

But things must have been very different from the point of view of Elizabethan audiences watching Shakespeare's King Lear for the first time. Henry VIII overturned the country based on the belief that a female heir would bring disaster, but he ended up leaving two female heirs in Mary and Elizabeth, both of whom became queen. Far from bearing out the historical prejudice, what happened instead was a golden age under the rule of Elizabeth. It was a decades-long period of economic, political, and cultural flourishing of which Shakespeare himself is arguably the greatest product. The audience at the King Lear premiere had lived through that. They could no longer believe the old dictum and probably viewed it as a bunch of superstitious nonsense. What they would have seen in the opening scene of the play was a silly old king whose hubristic nature leads him into a stupid decision that leads to disaster. For them, it must have been self-evident that Lear was at fault. That became the dominant interpretation that still exists in our time.

It's not hard to see why the Elizabethans would have understood the story in the way they did or why it has become the default interpretation. But, to say it again, this interpretation is wrong. More than that, Shakespeare seems to have deliberately created the misconception. Let's now start to unpack the covert exposition of the story to get to the bottom of the misunderstanding.

Setting aside the historical parallels and biases, it is still the case that Lear's lack of male heir in the story creates a problem he needs to solve. The rule of primogeniture still existed. If Lear had a male heir, the crown would automatically pass to him on Lear's death, and no special decision would be required. Because Lear has no male heir, he has to make other arrangements. He has three daughters. The eldest two are married, and the play begins with Gloucester and Kent speculating on which of the husbands Lear favours. Is it Albany or Cornwall? From the very beginning, the audience is primed for what was a very common issue in English royal politics.

By now we should know that Shakespeare never gives his hero a simple identity crisis to work through. On the contrary, in his greatest works, the Bard makes his hero lay everything on the line. Lear may be a king, but he is also a father. As a member of the royal family, his political and familial identities are combined. His eldest daughters, Goneril and Regan, have been married to what we presume are powerful English lords in Cornwall and Albany. We find out in the first scene that there are two suitors for the youngest daughter, Cordelia: the Duke of Burgundy and the King of France. Both of these make sense in terms of the marriage pattern of European royalty where marrying into foreign families was a normal tactic for creating political allegiance.

Thus, what we have at the beginning of the story is an ageing king who is taking care of two major pieces of business before he dies. By marrying off his youngest daughter, he is completing his responsibilities as a father. By announcing the succession of the throne, he is fulfilling his task as a king. This represents Lear in his holy state, the world he knows and is comfortable in. The king is seated on his throne, surrounded by the royal family and courtiers. He speaks and behaves with the authority of his position. He is making two decisions that everybody expects him to make. Yes, it is unusual that he doesn't have a son, but this is Elizabethan England where naming a daughter as an heir is no longer considered a curse and may very well be a blessing. Shakespeare gives us just a brief glimpse of the holy state before thrusting everybody into sacred state in one fell swoop.

Anybody familiar with the story knows what happens next. Lear announces his intention to give up the crown and make an "unburdened crawl towards death". He announces that the kingdom will be divided three ways, with a larger share going to whichever daughter loves him the most. This is an invitation to each to make a very public profession of their love before the entire court. Goneril and Regan take up the offer, making obsequious speeches in favour of their father. Cordelia refuses to play along. She says she loves Lear according to duty, the implication being that the public display of flattery is unseemly and against court etiquette. Lear flies into a rage. He disowns Cordelia. He announces that the kingdom will now be split two ways, one half for Goneril's husband Albany and the other for Regan's husband Cornwall. Kent objects, stating that Lear has gone mad. Lear banishes him. Burgundy and France are hauled in and told that there is a new deal on the table in relation to their potential bride. Since she has been disinherited, Cordelia no longer has a dowry, nor any connection to the royal line. Does either of them still want her? Burgundy declines. France agrees. He leaves with Cordelia. The scene ends.

We said earlier that the pace of Shakespeare's works is slow relative to modern storytelling. That is true in general, but there is perhaps no scene in all of the Bard's works where so much happens in such a short space of time as the opening sequence of King Lear. That should give us pause for thought. In fact, it is the exact advice that Kent gives to Lear in the scene itself. He tells the king to withhold his decision and think it over once the emotion of the moment has passed. Lear presses on anyway, seeming to get angrier and angrier. This is not behaviour fitting a king. It creates the impression that he really is going mad, exactly as Kent, Goneril, and Regan all remark.

It is the impression that the audience also receives and the one that guides understanding for the whole rest of the play. It is this initial impression that sits at the heart of the conventional understanding of the meaning of Lear, which has lasted more than four hundred years.

At this point, we must remember our earlier injunction that nothing can be ignored in Shakespeare. No speech or action is there by accident. Everything has a meaning. There are three things that Lear does in the opening scene that don't make sense. The last is the one that gets all the attention because it is the one that Cordelia refuses, namely, to flatter her father in front of the court. But that request is preceded by two other statements. Firstly, Lear says he is going to retire as king. Secondly, he will partition the kingdom into three.

Let's recall the problem that Lear faces. He has no male heir. Once upon a time, that would have been a major crisis. But Elizabethans knew better. Thus, even though the situation is unusual, there is a straightforward solution. Lear should just name his eldest daughter and her husband the sole heir of the kingdom. That is exactly what happened when Mary I was crowned. She was older than Elizabeth, and her claim took precedence. Thus, Lear is doing three things here that are unnecessary and against convention. The first is the famous flattery demand that everybody remembers. The other two have escaped attention.

Lear says he is going to retire early. That is a violation of the unspoken rule that the king is supposed to govern until he dies. This was another practice of English royal succession that had been around since time immemorial. Even if the king were senile, a caretaker would be found to manage the affairs of the kingdom. That had been done many times before and would be nothing unusual. Yet, Lear says he is going to give up the crown before dying. The second decision is that he is splitting the kingdom. That idea also has precedent from English history. It led to disaster when Henry II tried it.

Notice that the first two statements are about genuine affairs of state, while the flattery demand has nothing to do with the national interest and can only be understood as, at best, a personal quirk on Lear's part. Since the scene takes place in the formal setting of the court, personal business has no place there.

Thus, the first two statements should be the ones that get all the attention, but none of the other characters notice them because of the furore around the flattery demand, Cordelia's refusal, and Lear's eruption. The result is that they simply become accepted as what can and should happen. Lear is going to retire. He will divide his time between Goneril and Regan, who now have half the kingdom each. All of history suggests this is a terrible idea. *'A house divided cannot stand'* is one of the most famous quotes from Jesus for a reason. But these aspects of Lear's decision are quickly forgotten.

Lear is an old man. That much is clear. But we know that being king in the Shakespearean world is a very dangerous occupation. Hamlet's father is murdered. Macbeth kills Duncan. Othello and Leonato are targeted by the lies and deceits of Iago and Don John, respectively. Julius Caesar is assassinated by Brutus and the others. We could find many more examples. The fact that Lear has made it to old age tells us that he must have something going for him. Nevertheless, there seems to be no other reason for his decision. Nobody is trying to kill him. There is no immediate threat that he faces, no stress or other considerations that could explain why he is making what appears to be a very bad mistake. All of these facts lead to the explanation that he is going senile. What else could explain his behaviour?

To know what else could explain it, we must ask what the qualities of a good ruler are in Shakespeare's world. It is true that younger kings, like the rest of the nobility, were expected to receive military training and perhaps even to engage in combat. But this does not apply to older kings. Older kings must learn other skills. Shakespeare shows them to us in the story of Hamlet. Claudius is not on the throne because of superior physical strength but because of cunning and deceit. Not only was he able to poison Hamlet's father, he was able to cover up the crime. Even more impressively, he was able to create a story that enabled him to take the throne with seemingly no objection from anybody. Claudius wins support through charm on the one hand and covert operations on the other. Note how he engages Polonius, Guildenstern and Rosencrantz to be his spies. Note the secret letter to the English to have Hamlet killed. This is the way a Ruler must govern. The key word is 'covertly'.

What distinguishes Hamlet is that he knows how to play the game by

Claudius' rules. In fact, Hamlet may very well have learned how the game is to be played from his father. As the sole heir, he would no doubt have been receiving education for his eventual role as king, at least by being around the court to observe his father in action. In any case, Hamlet seems to know that the game is to be played covertly. He creates the illusion of madness to throw everybody off the scent of what he is doing. The only one who doesn't fall for his charade is Claudius. The story of Hamlet is the battle between two Rulers fought esoterically while the rest of the characters are oblivious to what is really going on.

And therein lies the key that will unlock our understanding of the true meaning of King Lear. What Lear is doing in the opening scene is creating an illusion, just like Hamlet does. And just as the other characters think that Hamlet has gone mad, so too does everybody think that Lear is going senile. That is what Kent tells him directly, and it is what Goneril and Regan whisper to each other at the close of Scene 1. The illusion worked. Lear wants everybody to think he has gone mad. The question we must now ask is, why? Lear has no enemy in the story. There is no Claudius to wage a covert war against. Why would he be creating such confusion and drama?

In order to answer that question, we must change our default assumptions about the character of Lear. We will no longer assume that he is the vainglorious, hot-tempered, half-senile fool that the opening sequence leads us to believe. Instead, let us imagine him as an older Hamlet. Let us believe he is a just and wise Ruler who has decades of experience playing the game of politics. Let us assume he wants to do what is best for his family and for the kingdom. Our new, wise Lear must be an excellent judge of character. In order to survive into old age, he must have learned how to spot the Iagos, the Claudiuses, and the Macbeths of this world. He must know the difference between them and the Othellos, the Desdemonas, and the Ophelias. He must be able to see what is in people's hearts.

If that is true, we can be very sure that Lear knows the character of his own daughters very well and also knows their husbands. What do we learn in the opening scene? We learn that Cordelia was Lear's favourite. What a coincidence that Lear just happens to know which of his daughters is virtuous.

And if he knows that, then he knows that the other two are not virtuous and will turn against their sisters at the first opportunity. He knows that Albany is a good but weak man, similar to Duncan in the story of Macbeth, and that Cornwall is an unscrupulous bastard, similar to Claudius and Iago. Since the story takes place in England, we can also assume that Lear is familiar with the history of royal succession and the problems caused when there is ambiguity and uncertainty over who will be heir.

All of sudden, the calculus that Lear faces with the issue of the succession of his kingdom changes enormously. Lear knows that Cordelia is the one who should be queen since she is the one who is virtuous. We might even imagine her as the female Hamlet. However, it would be completely against the rules to name Cordelia as heir. The rules say that the eldest receives the inheritance. That is true even in the unusual scenario where the heir is a daughter. We know from the events of the play that Goneril and Regan are not the kind of women who would passively accept the affront to their honour that would be the result of Cordelia being named. If Lear were to break all the rules and leave his kingdom to Cordelia, they may play along while he is alive, but they will turn on her as soon as he has gone, which is exactly what happens during the opening scene. Goneril and Regan are the ones who shamelessly flatter Lear and then plot against him in secret. If he knows their character well, he knows they will do the exact same thing to Cordelia if he names her queen. With the unscrupulous Cornwall waiting in the wings to take advantage of any weakness, this is a recipe for civil war. Therefore, Lear cannot simply make Cordelia queen.

What about the most obvious option, which is to name Goneril and Albany as the sole inheritors? This is the default option since Goneril is the eldest, but it also has obvious problems. Albany is a milksop. Cornwall is an ambitious psychopath. Without Lear as the authority figure, Goneril and Regan will quickly turn against each other. Knowing Cornwall, it is all but guaranteed that he would take the throne by force. Having killed Albany and possibly even Goneril, there is little chance he wouldn't also take out Cordelia too since she would be an heir to the throne and therefore a threat. It would be a Macbeth-style bloodbath. The exact same thing would happen if Lear simply made Regan and Cornwall king and queen. In that scenario, even if Albany were equanimous, Goneril would certainly become bitter, and Regan and Cornwall would never tolerate competitors who have a valid right to the throne.

If all of this sounds far-fetched, we must remember that it is exactly what happens in the story itself. As soon as Lear is removed from power, the two elder daughters and their husbands turn against each other. If we assume that Lear is a wise king who knows the characters of the four, it's easy to understand that he can foresee the crisis before it happens. Neither would any of this have been a surprise to Elizabethan audiences who would have expected these kinds of royal disputes because, again, it's exactly what happened with Henry VIII and his progeny. Before Elizabeth eventually began her long rule, there was all kinds of conflict between her and her older sister, Mary. Elizabeth was even briefly imprisoned by Mary after a failed rebellion attempt in which she was implicated. The idea that royal families would fight over the throne was not only not implausible; it was assumed. Quite possibly, the whole reason why strict rules around primogeniture were developed in the first place was to prevent the infighting which often turned into civil war. There is nothing implausible in the idea that Lear can foresee that, whichever way he hands over the kingdom, trouble looks certain to ensue. The reason why nobody has considered the idea is because the assumption has always been that Lear is half-mad. But Lear is just as clear-sighted as Hamlet and his plan is almost as intricate as Iago's. He knows exactly what he is doing.

Given our new understanding of Lear, we must also re-evaluate our earlier assumption that the story starts in holy state. It does so from an exoteric point of view in that Lear is still king and is still running the court according to his authority. But, esoterically, Lear must have been ruminating on the problem of succession for some time. The holy state for succession is primogeniture. That is the normal, safe, well-understood pathway. With that pathway unavailable, Lear is, by definition, in sacred state. Therefore, this is a sacred state that must have begun at the time when Lear realised it was too late to have any chance at a male heir. That is the first re-evaluation.

The second re-evaluation is that Lear's journey into the sacred is one that he is choosing for himself. What we see in the story of Lear is an identity crisis that we have so far only dealt with in its passive form as something that happens to the hero. Shakespeare has shown us several Father figures who deal with the crisis of how to hand over identity to the next generation – Leonato, Lord Capulet, King Hamlet, Duncan, and Brabantino. What do they all have in common? They all have only one child. As a result, when the child dies or is otherwise disinherited, the parents must grieve not just the loss of their loved one but the end of their lineage. However, in all these cases, the parent is forced into the identity crisis in a passive fashion. It is something that happens to them and which they react to, rather than something they initiate. What Shakespeare shows us in King Lear is a man who faces the identity crisis in an active fashion. That is why we can say that Lear is a true Shakespearean hero who is perfectly conscious of the problem that faces him and the sacrifice he needs to make to deal with it. He is the exact opposite of senile. The failure to understand this is the key error that has grounded four hundred years of incorrect interpretations of the story.

When we compare the identity crisis of Lear against other Father figures like Leonato and Lord Capulet, we see that Shakespeare has made a crucial innovation. The other parents we have mentioned have but one child. Lear may have three, but only one of them is virtuous. For all the other parents we have seen, their hopes for the child were not just born out of a desire to see their legacy live on but because they genuinely love and care for them. With Lear, we see something much more ambiguous and complex. Clearly, he loves and cares for Cordelia. But what about Goneril and Regan? Here, the test of love as flattery in the opening scene takes on a very different connotation which shows us something about the relationship between Lear and his daughters. We might be tempted to say that Goneril and Regan are flattering their father out of self-interest. But we must remember here the difference between love as duty and esoteric love. The concept of love was not seen to be entirely esoteric in Shakespeare's era. Doing your duty towards your loved ones was arguably more important. Thus, another way to look at the dynamic is that Goneril and Regan are upholding the honour of their father while Cordelia is not.

That would be true in any other circumstances, but the stakes in this case are so high that the obsequious display by the two daughters is beyond the pale, exactly as Kent points out. What this shows us is that Goneril and Regan lack the genuine love for their father that Cordelia has. This is the love that is predicated on wanting what is best for the loved one rather than hiding behind notions of honour and other exoteric facades. Lear's test of flattery shows who will uphold his exoteric honour no matter how badly he is acting. Goneril and Regan do that. In that respect, they are identical to Gertrude, Polonius, and the other courtiers in Hamlet who live entirely in the exoteric realm and will support whichever king happens to be sitting on the throne, even if he is a murderer and liar. Kent and Cordelia are the only ones who disagree. They are prepared to risk the honour of the king in order to do what is right for him and his kingdom.

Thus, another way to look at the distinction between Cordelia and her sisters is that she is the only one who has an esoteric understanding of virtue. She is the female equivalent of Hamlet. In trying to ensure that Cordelia is protected from future calamity, Lear is not just attempting to save his daughter; he is not just attempting to save his kingdom; he is attempting to ensure the transmission of esoteric virtue itself. What we see in the story of Lear is the father attempting to do what the elder generation of Montagues, Capulets, and Hamlets failed to do: ensure the full transmission of identity to the next generation.

Now we can grasp the full magnitude of the identity crisis that faces Lear. Goneril and Regan stand in the way of ensuring that Lear's inheritance may truly be handed down for posterity. That is true because they are both older than Cordelia and therefore have first right to the throne, and it is true because they do not understand esoteric and they will not accept the damage to their own honour that would be done by Lear raising Cordelia above them. If Lear wants Cordelia to take the throne, he must find a means to get her two sisters out of the way first. This is the problem that Lear is trying to solve when the play opens.

And now we are ready to understand the brilliant plan that Lear executes in the opening scene of the story. The first thing to note is that the two suitors for

Cordelia are both foreigners, while Goneril and Regan are married to English lords. Since a woman will live with her husband, the act of marrying her will remove Cordelia from England and put her out of harms way if a civil war starts. However, by the terms of the original three-way split, Cordelia would still own land in England, and that makes her a player in the politics of the kingdom. For Cordelia to be truly safe, she needs to be no threat to either of her sisters. The only way for that to happen is if she has no rights to the crown at all.

That brings us to the ridiculous flattery test. Lear knows his daughters well. He knows Goneril and Regan will acquiesce. He knows Cordelia will refuse. When Cordelia refuses, she is challenging Lear's honour. That gives him an excuse to fly off the handle. He gives her one more opportunity to repent, knowing she will fail. Now he really blows his top and disinherits her. The final step is to marry her off. Burgundy and France are brought in. The former was only interested in Cordelia for her wealth. The latter was genuinely in love with her. That's why Burgundy declines the marriage and France accepts. In one fell swoop, Lear has ensured that Cordelia is out of the country, married to a man who genuinely cares for her, and is no longer a political threat to either of her sisters. The scene where everybody believes that Lear has gone mad is actually a triumph of the first order. Lear's plan has gone exactly as he wanted it to. He has saved his favourite daughter.

The flattery test has nothing to do with Lear's personality or supposed senility at all. It is a perfectly calculated tactic that allows him to disinherit Cordelia. But it's even more brilliant than that because the test also creates the chaos that sees the first two of Lear's announcements go completely unnoticed. These reveal that Lear's plan expands beyond just ensuring that Cordelia is safely overseas.

The first announcement is that Lear is going to retire. It's worth reiterating that this was unheard of at the time. The king reigned until he died. Even if he was completely senile, a caretaker would be found to run the affairs of state until the crown could be handed over formally to the nominated heir. Why does Lear want to take such an unprecedented step of retiring early? And why does he proceed to split the kingdom no longer three ways but only two?

The answer can only be that Lear wants to bring matters to a head. Rather than put off the strife until after he is dead, Lear is bringing it forward. He is betting that his two daughters and their husbands will not be able to resist the use of the power that they have now been entrusted with. But he is going to do more than that. He is going to actively attempt to create the civil war himself by turning his daughters and their husbands against each other.. Working through the details of this would take us too far astray from our analysis; therefore, this can be left as an exercise for the reader. To see how Lear encourages war between Albany and Cornwall, watch his actions starting in Act 1 – Scene 3 and ending in Act 2 – Scene 4. Note: Very close attention must be paid to what is shown and implied, especially in relation to the letter that Lear sends to Regan.

From this, we can deduce Lear's grand plan. He removed Cordelia from the country in order to provoke the war that he knows will happen anyway between Albany and Cornwall. The fact that Lear has retained one hundred knights allows him to re-establish order or tilt the war in whichever direction he wants. In either case, it means he can take back power afterwards and that would open the way for Cordelia to take the throne. If the plan succeeds, Lear will have protected Cordelia, solved the succession problem, and ensured the stability of the kingdom. Far from being the story of a half-senile old king who loses the plot, King Lear is about a man who faces the greatest challenge of any of Shakespeare's heroes and constructs a brilliant plan to attempt to solve it.

Of course, the plan does not succeed, and that is the brutal truth that Lear must face as the story rolls on. But, even before the question of success or failure is raised, we must acknowledge that this plan is deeply morally ambiguous. Lear is attempting to curtail a civil war by creating a civil war, one that will put numerous people in harm's way. It may seem hard to believe, but the other Shakespearean hero that Lear has most in common with is Iago. Why? Well, first of all, Lear's plan is an extended and highly risky deception that requires Lear to pursue a secret agenda while he maintains the exoteric façade of something very different. There are two main differences between the men. Firstly, Iago was acting out of hatred with the intent to destroy. Lear is acting out of love with the intention to preserve. Secondly, Lear is putting himself through a genuine transformation, one that requires him to create a role that has never existed before. Kings do not retire for the very reason that it creates ambiguity and uncertainty in the chain of command. The only way Lear gets away with such a preposterous suggestion is by creating the furore around Cordelia's banishment. He creates for himself a brand new exoteric role that nobody else can understand because it has no precedent. That is a big part of the reason why he is seen to be mad. Nobody knows how to deal with a retired king. Nevertheless, Lear manages to use this role to pursue an esoteric agenda that nobody else in the story is aware of. That is why he is similar to Iago.

Of course, the other difference between the two is that Lear fails in his plan, whereas Iago succeeds. The bitter irony is that it is not his enemies who bring Lear down, because he has none. Instead, it is his family and his closest ally, Kent, who ruin the plan. The reason that happens is because none of them understand what the plan is. Lear is unable to take anybody into his confidence. In that respect, he is not just like Iago but also Hamlet. Recall that Hamlet's great existential crisis comes from him realising that the court and the people in it, including his own mother and uncle, operate entirely according to exoteric appearances. Nobody truly grieves the late king because nobody truly understood or cared for him at the esoteric level. The same applies to Lear. And that is why he must operate entirely alone. There is nobody in whom he can confide, nobody with whom he has an esoteric relationship capable of the levels of trust and intimacy required.

It's worthwhile summarising why this is the case. Obviously, Lear cannot confide in Goneril and Regan since they would have to give up the throne willingly and that is not something they or their husbands would do. We might think that Lear could confide in Kent, who is loyal to a fault. But Kent is a man who lives entirely in the world of honour, which is to say, entirely in the exoteric. Lear's plan is devious in nature. A man like Kent would be honour-bound to reject it. What about Gloucester? He is far too naïve and trusting. It is his lack of discretion that empowers Edmund later in the story. If Lear confides in Gloucester, he can count on the plan being leaked, and that would ruin everything.

Finally, there is Cordelia. And here we come to the real issue because it is Cordelia who is virtuous, and we have assumed it is she who should reign for that reason. Who wouldn't want a virtuous queen on the throne? It is self-evident that Lear embodies the Ruler archetype, and we have seen that the whole problem that he faces is that there is no obvious candidate to inherit his position. That doesn't mean there is nobody to take the exoteric role; it means that there is nobody who could take the role and not cause an immediate crisis after Lear is dead. We know that Goneril and Regan are not up to the job because we see from the action of the story that they will turn against each other. Lear is correct in that. However, there is a fatal flaw in Lear's plan, and it relates to the problem of what makes a good Ruler. Cordelia is a paragon of virtue, but virtue is not enough. A Ruler must be willing and able to do things that would be counted by the average person as vices. Lear's own plan is a perfect example of that because it involves a deception of the highest order. Moreover, it involves Lear creating a crisis. He may be doing so in order to ward off future problems that are going to happen anyway, but by creating his own crisis he takes the responsibility on himself. Of course, that is what a true Ruler must do. A Ruler must be prepared to lie, deceive, and even kill where necessary.

Lear's desire to protect Cordelia, while understandable and honourable in itself, means that he is not initiating her into the realities of what it means to be a Ruler. But we might frame the issue in starker terms. Cordelia's purity means that she is no better suited to become a Ruler than either of her sisters. For all their faults, Goneril and Regan are prepared to actually show some leadership when it is required. They are prepared even to sacrifice their own father. Cordelia is not prepared to sacrifice her virtue. That is what we learn in the opening scene. She will do what is right even when it is inexpedient and removes her from power. The bitter irony is that she is just as ill-suited as her sisters for a position as Ruler. The fact that Lear cannot confide in her about his plans demonstrates that fact. If she was truly capable of leadership, Lear could have made her his partner. But he cannot.

This is no mere philosophical speculation. Shakespeare bakes this dynamic into the heart of the story. It becomes the main point which ruins Lear's plan and brings about the tragic ending. If Lear could have told Cordelia his plan, then he could have got her to agree to stay in France until the war between Albany and Cornwall was over. But he does not confide in her. What happens? The loyal-to-a-fault Kent, now banished from the kingdom, organises with Cordelia to launch an attack to try and save Lear. Lear's whole plan was to drive a wedge between Albany and Cornwall and cause them to fight each other. Instead, they are brought together in order to fight a foreign enemy. It is Kent's loyalty and Cordelia's virtue which bring this state of affairs about. Lear's plan and his kingdom are brought undone not just by vice but by virtue. A true Ruler must be in command of both.

This insight sheds new light on the story of Hamlet. We have said that Hamlet and Cordelia are similar in their virtuous nature, by which we mean that they are both attuned to the esoteric aspect of life in contrast to those around them who live entirely in the exoteric world. Hamlet pursues the virtues of truth and justice but does so in an entirely esoteric fashion, believing that this will be enough to secure the right outcome. He is ultimately defeated by Claudius, who is not in touch with the esoteric side of his character but knows what it takes to operate in the real world of court politics. Claudius was prepared to do what was necessary to take power. Hamlet was not. The result was the destruction of the entire royal family. This outcome could have been prevented if Hamlet had acted when he had the chance to kill Claudius. But Hamlet was not prepared to sacrifice virtue for power.

Lear has no such qualms. The entire opening sequence is a deceit that fools everybody. His plan risks a bloody war in which his own daughters bear no insignificant risk. As part of that plan, he insults his daughters to their faces. He is indirectly responsible for the rise of Edmund and the fall of Gloucester, not to mention the other calamities that occur. The only redeeming factor in all of this is that the events that play out prove exactly why he needed to act. Rather than let destruction befall the kingdom after he is gone, Lear takes the responsibility on himself and makes one final attempt to set things in order. Ultimately, that is the greatest virtue of the Ruler: to take responsibility for the most difficult decisions whose outcome can never be known in advance.

Since every major decision has good and bad consequences, it follows that the leader must take responsibility for both. The great challenge for every Ruler is not to lose sight of virtue while engaging in vice. Lear may be practising vice, but he does so while keeping his eyes firmly on virtue. That is what makes him arguably the greatest Ruler in literature.

As with all of Shakespeare's other great tragedies, Lear's attempt ultimately fails, and, just like in Hamlet, the disaster destroys the entire family line. We have barely touched on the main body of the story itself, and it is not our purpose here to do so. However, in conclusion, there is one last point to make about the way in which Shakespeare ends the story. We know to expect that there will be one or more witnesses to the tragedy. In Romeo and Juliet, this was Friar Lawrence and the parents. In Hamlet, it was Horatio. In Macbeth, it was Macduff and Malcolm. In Othello, it was Emilia. In King Lear, those who bear witness to the tragedy are also those who will carry things forward in its aftermath.

We have seen several times already that Shakespeare will provide a second hero or group of characters that serves as a comparison in the story. For example, Emilia and Iago are the married couple to be compared with Othello and Desdemona. Benedick and Beatrice are to be compared with Hero and Claudio in Much Ado About Nothing. In Lear, we have the royal family with an ageing father, no sons, and three daughters. Of the daughters, only one is virtuous. There is a second family in the story with Gloucester as the patriarch. He is about the same age as Lear, but he has two sons and no daughters. Of the sons, one is virtuous but naïve. The other is ambitious, adaptive, and calculating. Unlike the Lear family, however, it is the eldest son, and therefore heir, Edgar who is virtuous, while the younger, Edmund, is where the trouble lies. That trouble is also based around the question of inheritance because Edmund is in the position familiar to the younger aristocratic sons of the era in that he can expect to receive almost no inheritance since everything will go to the eldest son. Edmund also has extra reason for grievance since he is a bastard who was conceived by his father and a prostitute. This gives us some insight into Gloucester's character, although it is to his credit that the earl has agreed to support Edmund rather than abandon him as was so often the case in these circumstances.

In actual fact, Edmund appears in the opening minutes of the play, a fact easily forgotten by the dramatic events which occur shortly thereafter. When the action begins, we see Gloucester introducing him to Kent. Kent is accommodating and tells the younger man he would like to get to know him. Edmund reciprocates. What we are shown here is the beginning of an Orphan-Elder relationship. Kent is set to become a mentor to Edmund, to introduce and educate him in the ways of the court. Since we learn that Edmund has already spent many years away from home travelling, he is the perfect exemplar of an Orphan who has already begun the process of creating an identity for himself.

It is this which separates Edmund from his half-brother Edgar. As the son and heir, Edgar has been trapped in the household of his father. As a result, he lacks worldly experience, especially because Gloucester is also quite naïve. That is why Edmund will later be able to easily fool them both. The fact that he does so is another unintended side effect of Lear's plan. Kent should have become a mentor to Edmund. He could have then guided his talents into serving the court. But Kent gets banished from the kingdom, and Edmund is left to his own devices. Rather than being initiated into an existing institution by an experienced campaigner, Edmund must create a place of his own in the new court that now consists of Goneril and Regan. He will do so by betraying his father and brother in exactly the same way that Goneril and Regan will betray Lear. No surprises, then, to find that both Goneril and Regan end up falling for Edmund later in the story.

If Edmund is the counterpart to Goneril and Regan, then we may say that Edgar corresponds to Cordelia. That is true in that both of them are virtuous, honest, naive. But the journey that Edgar must go through is very different, and it is ultimately Edgar and not Cordelia who is left to pick up the pieces at the end of the play. In fact, Edgar will become the son that Lear never had and will be his true inheritor.

Let's do a lightning review of Edgar's story. His holy state at the beginning is still to be in the Child archetype. He is living comfortably under the roof of his father with little to no real-world experience. Presumably, the nation has also been at peace for some time, and that is why the domestic atmosphere is relaxed. It is Edmund who will throw Edgar out of his holy state and into the sacred by manufacturing a deceit in which he fools Gloucester into thinking Edgar is trying to have him killed. So convincing is Edmund that Gloucester tries to have Edgar arrested. He is forced to flee for his life and has a bounty placed on his head. Note the symbolism here. The Child has now been cut off from the father and forced out of the house. This is Edgar's Orphan transition, albeit one that is conducted in highly unusual and stressful circumstances. Just like Hamlet, Edgar's exoteric identity has been completely destroyed, and he is thrown back into the esoteric. He takes on the appearance of a crazy beggar in order to avoid detection by the authorities (just as Hamlet pretends to be mad).

At exactly the same time that Edgar has been transitioned into the Orphan archetype, Lear has also had his exoteric identity destroyed by his daughters. Just like Edgar, Lear is thrown out of Gloucester's house. The two of them meet in a shack on the moor, where they seek shelter from the storm which is raging. The great king who is pretending to be mad meets the young man who is also pretending to be mad. Lear becomes the Elder to Edgar's Orphan. Of course, there is no question of an exoteric initiation because both of them have been stripped of their exoteric identity. What Edgar will experience is an induction into the esoteric directly, a view of what man is when he is cut off from society, and a lesson in what it means when the authority of the Ruler gives way to chaos and bloodshed.

Both men have entered the sacred state in its purest form. Their worldly, exoteric identity is dissolved, and they are thrown back onto something more fundamental. That fundamental is the esoteric itself. The esoteric, by definition, cannot be directly observed in others. All we may do is to infer it. Our ability to perceive it can come only through our own experience of it. Lear has been through the esoteric before. His raging against the storm is not madness. It is defiance. As he himself says, whatever the world may throw at us in the form of nature is a trifle compared to the confrontation with the sacred. Lear says he will remain in the storm because it distracts him from something worse: the sacred.

Prior to this, Edgar was in the shelter alone. His own exoteric identity has been destroyed. Now the man who only recently possessed the highest exoteric identity in the land stands before him. Edgar has become the witness to Lear's journey into the sacred, which mirrors his own. It is in this way that Lear becomes the esoteric Elder to Edgar when previously he had been only an exoteric figure (king).

What Edmund already knows, and what Edgar must learn, is that the older generation is not infallible. That is also part of the transition from Child to Adult. As children, we worship our parents as gods. It is a difficult transformation to realise that this is not the case. The cynicism of the Orphan is born out of this. In psychological terms, the Orphan projects the pain caused by the sacred state back onto the Parent. They may blame the Parent and desire to take retribution. They may try to overthrow the Parent and take power for themselves. That is the pathway taken by Edmund, Goneril, and Regan.

Edgar shows us another way. Although he has every reason to be bitter and resentful against his own father, whose gullibility has caused Edgar's life to be thrown into chaos, the thought never occurs to him. Indeed, the pathway Edgar ends up taking is that of forgiveness and esoteric understanding. It is no coincidence that his reunion with his father occurs immediately after Edgar's meeting with Lear in the shelter. Edgar now sees his father with new eyes, no longer as a god but as a man.

In the meantime, Gloucester has received his own punishment. His gullibility and ignorance are symbolised by the removal of his eyes by Cornwall and Regan. Edgar meets him on his journey to Dover. The son comes face-to-face with his father, who is no longer anything resembling a god but a broken man. Edgar becomes his guide and protector. In the void left by the loss of Lear's authority over the nation and his father's authority over his family, Edgar steps into a new role. The Orphan's transformation is no longer to blindly follow authority as a Child does. It is to do what is right for its own sake. In that respect, Edgar is very similar to Hamlet but with the big difference that the battle that comes at the end is one that Edgar chooses and then wins.

Edgar initiates a duel with Edmund. He puts on knight's armour, not because it was given to him, but because he chooses to wear it. He has now graduated from Orphan into the role of Warrior, fighting not on behalf of any king or formal authority, because there isn't one left, but on behalf of virtue itself. Edgar is prepared to sacrifice his life in the name of virtue despite the fact that he has nothing to gain in doing so. In that way, he is the opposite of Iago and also of Edmund, whose actions have been driven by unregulated self-interest. Edgar is driven by a higher calling discovered not in the court of the king with all its exoteric pomp and ceremony but on the heath during a torrential storm when he saw Lear for the man that he really is.

We have seen numerous examples of intergenerational conflict in this book. There are the troubles between Leonato and his daughter; the Capulets and Montagues come to ruin; the house of Hamlet is destroyed. In all those cases, we are inclined to blame the older generation for the carnage. In King Lear, we have an example of the younger generation being at fault via the actions of Edmund, Goneril, and Regan who destroy their parents. Of course, Lear had tried desperately to avoid that outcome. Despite his best intentions, his brilliant plan cannot save his own household from ruin.

Nevertheless, the story of King Lear shows us an intergenerational transfer in the esoteric domain. It is not achieved through the holy state of ceremonies, rites, and laws, but through a journey into the sacred. Lear chooses to destroy his own exoteric identity in a bid to save Cordelia and his kingdom. Although he fails in that goal, his journey sets the example for Edgar. It is Edgar who becomes Lear's witness and his true inheritor, and this is fitting because it was Lear's journey into the sacred which triggered the events that led Edgar to find himself in the same position, stripped of all the exoteric aspects of his identity and thrown back onto the pure esoteric. By inadvertently putting Edgar through this initiation, Lear creates his true successor.

However, Lear does not survive to understand that. Instead, he is made to experience the pain of losing the very thing he had set out to protect. The reunion with Cordelia at the end of the play, where for a brief moment it seems that the old man may be able to genuinely retire and enjoy the company of his favourite daughter, is cut short by Edmund. As Lear grieves her loss, he is consoled by Kent. He turns to him and the others and shouts:

> *"A plague upon you murderers, traitors all!* ***I might have saved her****;*
> *now she's gone forever." (emphasis mine)*

Lear dies shortly thereafter, and Shakespeare gives the final words of the play to Edgar, the king's witness and true inheritor:-

> *The weight of this time we must obey;*
> *Speak what we feel, not what we ought to say.*
> *The oldest hath borne most; we that are young*
> *Shall never see so much nor live so long.*

Speak what we feel, not what we ought to say. This is an injunction to share the esoteric truth, something which Lear had been unable to do, not even with Cordelia. Far from being a work of nihilism, King Lear is Shakespeare's greatest affirmation of truth, integrity, and, above all, honesty.

The Tempest

The Tempest is a self-portrait. Various commentators down through the centuries have flirted with this interpretation to differing degrees, but within the interpretative framework we have been using in this book, it is crystal clear. This fact would be poignant enough in itself, but it takes on far greater significance when we consider that The Tempest was also Shakespeare's final work and that the Bard was only in his late forties when he wrote it. Although he died only a few years later, there was no indication of ill health at the time of writing. Thus, Shakespeare followed the example of King Lear by retiring early. His swan song is not just a self-portrait; it is also a kind of "greatest hits" collection that pays homage to all the main themes we have covered in this book. Most importantly, it is his primary meditation on the meaning and power of art and the role he saw for it in the development of the highest forms of humanity.

To begin to unpack the meanings of the work, we may begin with the aspects of the story that are different from any we have seen so far. The first of these is the archetype of the hero. Although Prospero is a magician in the story, we will characterise him as belonging to the Sage archetype. The Sage is concerned with the deeper truths of life. In the Western tradition, our foremost exemplars of the Sage have been the priest, the philosopher, and the scientist. Against this cultural background, the fact that Prospero is a magician may seem problematic. Priests, philosophers, and scientists down through the ages have all been agreed on one thing, and that is that magic, to the extent that it is even considered to exist, is the opposite of truth. Well, we know by now what Shakespeare thought of philosophers. In any case, the magic in the story is quite obviously a metaphor for art. Prospero stands for Shakespeare, and magic stands for his art.

Because we are still the inheritors of the Romantic tradition which began in the 19th century, we are far more likely to at least accept the idea that the artist can be a Sage, and we should remember again that Shakespeare was arguably the number one influence on the Romantic ideal. If so, then The Tempest should rank as his major contribution to that idea since he presents us with the magician-as-Sage in the form of Prospero. The implied claim is that illusion can be more truthful than the "truth" by representing back to us those parts of reality which the priests, philosophers, and scientists have ignored. This part of reality is what we have called the sacred. It is during the sacred part of the transformation cycle that the world becomes weird and our categories of truth break down. Prospero-as-magician mirrors Shakespeare-as-artist in not shying away from these aspects of reality but embracing and mastering them. Thus, The Tempest is not just unique within Shakespeare's *oeuvre*; it may be the very first work of what would later be called Romanticism.

Against these lofty themes, it may seem strange to find that The Tempest is really a quite light-hearted comedy, not in the sense that it contains many jokes and witticisms, but in the sense that there is a happy ending. It is also true that the story seems to lack the emotional depth that we have become used to. There is little to no drama at all because Prospero is an all-powerful character who controls everything that happens throughout. The other characters therefore have far less agency and depth than we are used to in Shakespeare.

The reason for this is that The Tempest is a work of symbolism. The characters and events get their meaning as pointers to something else. Prospero is a pointer to Shakespeare. The other characters are partly symbols of archetypes we have already seen in other works. That is what allows The Tempest to function as a summary of Shakespeare's *oeuvre*. But the symbolism in the work is multi-faceted, meaning that every character is a pointer to multiple meanings. A prime example is the character of Miranda and her love interest Ferdinand. Miranda is the daughter of Prospero. If

Prospero stands for Shakespeare, then who does Miranda stand for? The answer is Shakespeare's audience – us. One of the things Shakespeare is doing in The Tempest is showing us how his art functions. The characters in the story are manipulated by Prospero in the same way that the playwright manipulates his own creations. The Tempest is full of meta-meanings that we need to understand symbolically.

The symbolic nature of the work can also be seen in another crucial difference between The Tempest and the other stories we have investigated. The majority of our analysis in this book has been about unpacking the covert exposition that Shakespeare uses so expertly. All of the plays we have looked at have used covert exposition to some extent, and, in the case of Hamlet and King Lear, it is only once we grasp it that the true meaning of the works can be understood. Can it be a coincidence then that Shakespeare chose to use not covert but overt exposition at the beginning of The Tempest? Can it be a further coincidence that the overt exposition is very lengthy and cannot be missed? Finally, can it be a coincidence that the character who gives the exposition is the one who stands for Shakespeare (Prospero) and the one who receives it is the one who stands for us (Miranda)? We know by now that there are no coincidences in Shakespeare. Everything has meaning. The question then is, what is the meaning of this?

The standard methods of exposition, used countless times in works of fiction, are a narrator who tells us directly what is going on and a character who does the same via dialogue or thought. In The Tempest, Shakespeare employs the second method by having Prospero explain to his daughter Miranda the last twelve years of both of their lives. Miranda is just emerging from childhood. Within the logic of the story, we have a father telling his daughter the truth about her life now that he believes she is old enough to understand. But Miranda stands for us, the audience, and Prospero stands for Shakespeare. Therefore, Shakespeare is telling us that we are now ready to understand how his art works. The overt exposition at the beginning of the story mirrors the symbolic nature of the whole work. Shakespeare is making overt what until now has been covert. That is why in The Tempest nothing is hidden or esoteric. Prospero guides all events from his mountaintop, effortlessly pulling the strings, making characters do what he wants, contriving situations, and resolving everything as he wishes. Shakespeare is telling us that this is how art works. He trusts that we are now ready to understand the truth.

With that in mind, let's now explore the truths contained within Shakespeare's final work.

***

The Tempest begins with, well, a tempest. A storm seemingly destroys a shipload of people, including five men of rank. There is a family group: Alonso the king of Naples, his brother Sebastian, and his son Ferdinand. Then there is Antonio the Duke of Milan and his elderly courtier Gonzalo. But, as with everything in the story, the storm was no random freak of nature. Immediately after the dramatic events on board, we see Prospero and his daughter Miranda on a hilltop overlooking the carnage. Prospero has used his magic to cause the shipwreck. Miranda wonders why, and we get the long exposition that tells the backstory of both. Prospero explains that he was once the duke of Milan, and his brother Antonio teamed up with Alonso to steal the title from him. Prospero and Miranda were thrown into a ship and left for dead. They somehow survived and ultimately ended up on the island where they have been living for the last twelve years.

As usual, Shakespeare begins the story with an immediate transition from holy state to sacred state. The crew on board the ship, including the five noblemen, are thrown into danger and expect to die. More subtly, the fact that Prospero is conducting his magic in front of Miranda is a deliberate choice on his part. We know this because he easily hides his activities from her later. Something has changed in their relationship. Miranda is finding out that her father is something more than just a man who lives in a cave. He used to be a nobleman, and that means that she should rightfully be a noblewoman.

In our archetypal terminology, what we have is a Father-Daughter pairing that is about to change because the young lady has come of age. The reason there are no Child heroes in Shakespeare is because he assumes what was generally believed to be true in that era, which is that children are ignorant of the real world. It is only once they hit puberty, otherwise called the *age of reason*, that they are capable of understanding. By showing his daughter his magic, Prospero is acknowledging that she has reached the age where she can understand. The event marks her transition from Child to Orphan. The sacrifice she must make is to give up the blissful ignorance of childhood and begin to understand the world in its good and bad aspects. That also includes a fuller understanding of the kind of man her father is.

Miranda is transitioning to sacred state. The men who are shipwrecked are most definitely in sacred state too. What about Prospero? Well, the arrival of his enemies also means that he is about to leave the holy state that he has been in for the last twelve years, wherein he was able to perfect his magic while raising his daughter. The sacrifice he is going to have to make is to give up his life on the island. He's also going to give up the role of being Miranda's guardian, since she is going to get married. All of this ties back to the overarching metaphor that is at play in the story. Shakespeare is giving up his art. We, the audience, are in the role of Miranda, and we are now "old enough" to be able to understand rationally what we have previously only experienced subjectively. In that respect, you might say we are also in sacred state in that we need to approach The Tempest differently than we have learned to understand Shakespeare's other works.

As for the men in the ship, Prospero has just made them experience what they put him and Miranda through twelve years earlier. This gives us our first glimpse into one of the meanings of art that Shakespeare is communicating with the work, namely, its ability to mirror reality back to us and thereby to make people understand the consequences of their own actions. What Prospero is trying to do is to make holy a violation that had occurred twelve years earlier. In this respect, Prospero has been in sacred state for the whole time, estranged from his home and devoid of his true title and role in society. He is going to return to holy state by making the truth known to his enemies via magic and illusion. This is a concept we have seen already. It is what Hamlet attempts in relation to Claudius by having his actors mirror the king's actions back to him directly. Shakespeare implies that art can be a trigger for the conscience of those who have done wrong and thereby a redemptive act not just for the perpetrators but also for the artist himself.

Here we need to slightly correct our use of the term "illusion", and we can do so by reference to the concept we have been using throughout this book: the esoteric. Art is esoteric in nature. So, too, are philosophical concepts such as truth, conscience, redemption, and justice. The Sage archetype is primarily concerned with the esoteric aspects of existence. The modern bias is that these esoteric aspects are less real than material reality, which is what we have been calling the exoteric. It is definitely true that the exoteric elements of reality are more general and widely understood. In almost every Shakespeare story, there is a dichotomy between those characters who are in tune with the esoteric and those who can only see the exoteric. That is the central problem that faces Hamlet. It is why King Lear is seen to be mad. The Sage sees the esoteric as not only not illusory but as the most important aspect of existence. Shakespeare encapsulates his version of this with the most famous line from The Tempest – "We are such stuff as dreams are made on". Is the dream an illusion, or is it the most real thing there is? That depends on whether you understand the Sage. That depends on whether you have learned to see the esoteric.

There are three groups of characters in The Tempest who differ in how they are attuned to the esoteric, the effect it has on them, and the result that Prospero wishes to induce. We can easily recognise each group from previous works. First, there is the pair of young lovers. Prospero sees to it that Alonso's young son, Ferdinand, washes ashore alone and happens to meet Miranda. They fall in love at first sight, a direct reference to Claudio and Hero, Benedick and Beatrice, Romeo and Juliet, and Hamlet and Ophelia. Since this kind of love is esoteric by default, we can say that this group is already attuned to the esoteric aspect of existence.

The second group are the noblemen, including the two who betrayed Prospero, Alonso and Antonio. Also included is the courtier, Gonzalo, who bears a striking resemblance to Polonius in the story of Hamlet. What is going to happen to this group is also a story we have seen many times in this book. Sebastian is going to conspire with Antonio to kill his brother and take the crown, just as Antonio had conspired with Alonso to do the same to Prospero twelve years earlier. The main vice of these characters is unchecked ambition that is strong enough to override even familial bonds. We have seen it already in Macbeth, Lady Macbeth, Goneril, Regan, Edmund, and Claudius. This group's primary attunement to the esoteric is via the conscience that should provide a check on their ambition or, at least, allow them the prospect of redemption afterward.

The final group is an assortment of depraved lower-class characters. The first is Caliban, who was on the island when Prospero first arrived. He is the ugly, misshapen son of a witch who Prospero treated well for years until he tried to rape Miranda. Caliban is the barely human representation of vice, similar to the witches in Macbeth. Prospero teams him up with two of the king's servants who had been separated from their master in the shipwreck. There is the jester, Trinculo, and the butler, Stephano. Stephano has a virtually unlimited supply of wine due to the barrel that he rode ashore on. He and the others proceed to get rolling drunk. Caliban comes up with a plan to kill Prospero and take over the island and convinces the others to help him. This group represents all of Shakespeare's characters who are filled with bitterness, resentment, greed, and lust, which they use as motivation to destroy. Representatives include Iago, Roderigo, Edmund, and Don John. This group's attunement to the esoteric is entirely an extension of their will. They deceive esoterically but do not believe in the higher forms of love, justice, or truth.

This is what is meant when we say that The Tempest is a kind of "greatest hits" compilation befitting its status as Shakespeare's swan song. But there is another unique thing that Shakespeare does in the story. In previous works, almost all of the characters from the three groups just mentioned are tragic ones who come to grief by the end of the story. What happens in The Tempest is that Prospero guides them all to a happy conclusion. He does so by ensuring that the elements of their character that bring them undone are corrected by the guiding hand of the Sage. This is the second meta-meaning about the purpose of art which Shakespeare is communicating, although it fits perfectly with the traditional notion of the Sage archetype as the repository of wisdom.

The important part is that Prospero is not himself aloof from all this. His ability to steer things right only comes out of the real life experience he has had to endure, his own journey into the sacred.

Perhaps the most amusing example of Prospero guiding the other characters towards a happy outcome is the love story between Ferdinand and Miranda. Having arranged the marriage of the two lovers, Prospero instructs Ferdinand not to try and sleep with Miranda until after the marriage ceremony. He then sends the two into the cave while he attends to other business, clearly a major temptation to a couple of horny teenagers. Not only do the youngsters not take the bait, but the next time we see them, they are playing a cordial and perfectly chaste game of chess. This is the world as it would look if guided by the wise hand of the Sage.

The way in which Prospero ruins the plans of the bitter and resentful revolutionaries is equally amusing. He allows them to make their way to his cave, where they stand on the threshold of victory. But he hangs some gaudy clothing on a line nearby, which is enough to distract Trinculo and Stephano, whose main vice is not really hatred or lust for power but greed. They are easily neutralised with the promise of free stuff. Caliban is the one who is driven by hate, and he has no interest in the clothing. He is incensed that the other two refuse to help him when the real goal is right before them. All three of them are then easily scared away with the help of another of Prospero's illusions.

The final group is the one which caused Prospero to become a magician in the first place by stealing his title as Duke of Milan. There is nothing subtle about Prospero's approach to them. He has the spirit Ariel confront them in the form of a monster and tell them their sins directly. We may contrast this with the incredibly subtle inner battle that Macbeth undergoes over the question of whether to kill Duncan or Hamlet's famous to-be-or-not-to-be soliloquy. Alonso and the others clearly do not possess an inner conscience in this fashion. If they did, it would have already been activated. Instead, they must be confronted with their crimes in an overt fashion. They are thereafter forced to wander in a maze, stuck in a kind of purgatory created by Prospero.

For the first group of lovers, Prospero manages to convince them not to spoil their esoteric love by the pleasures of the flesh. For the second group, the esoteric is nothing more than an illusion meant to terrify the no-gooders into submission. For the third group, the esoteric is a trigger for the action of conscience, a way to mirror the actions of the men back to themselves so that they may realise the error of their ways.

All this is true at the same time that the story itself shows us characters who are little more than puppets on a string dancing to the tune set by Prospero. This comes back to the meta meaning that Shakespeare is conveying that this is how art works. The artist is Prospero, and he has complete control over events. This would be a shallow and trivial tale if it weren't for the fact that we already know these characters. It is precisely because Shakespeare has already painted them in detail in his other works that he can now utilise them as symbols. But the key point to understand is that the symbols are multi-faceted. The three groups refer back to the characters in Shakespeare's other works and their own attunement to the esoteric. But they also point to the real world because those characters are portraits of the kinds of people that really exist. The Tempest gives us a meta spectacle. We are an audience watching the artist create "art" for the characters in the story, who are therefore also an audience. The symbolism therefore extends to the way in which Shakespeare sees his art being understood by his own audience.

Let's consider the young couple Miranda and Ferdinand. They represent the audience that Shakespeare is most directly addressing. They are the ones who are attuned to the highest forms of the esoteric and who are now "old enough" to finally understand his art. We have already seen that the story opens with Prospero demonstrating his magic to Miranda for the first time. Later on, after Ferdinand and Miranda have been married, Prospero creates another illusion for both of them. He tells them directly that this is magic and that its purpose is to consecrate their marriage by bestowing the blessings of various gods and goddesses. As the show continues, Ferdinand gets carried away. Bedazzled by the spectacle, he wants to stay in the illusion forever:

> *"Let me live here ever; So rare a wond'red father and wise makes this place paradise."*

There then occurs a crucial event that tells us much about Shakespeare's attitude to art and the esoteric more generally. The show that Prospero is putting on gets interrupted because the three revolutionaries have almost found their way to the cave. The basis of Prospero's power and authority is about to be lost, and he must turn away from the beautiful aspects of life to take care of it. Art and the esoteric may be the highest thing in life, but it cannot eliminate vice or any of the baser instincts of mankind. We are not free to renounce the exoteric and live forever in the esoteric. Attunement to the esoteric cannot come at the expense of the lower forms of life because those lower forms will rise up and destroy it.

This is the primary potential failing of the Sage archetype, the desire to lose oneself in the esoteric and disconnect from the "real world". The Sage must never forget the difference between the esoteric and exoteric and must not ignore the latter to indulge in the former. This lesson has already been communicated in numerous other stories. Othello is fooled by the illusions of Iago. All the other characters in Much Ado About Nothing are tricked by Don John. King Lear pulls the wool over everybody's eyes. The risk of the esoteric is that it does become an illusion. Another way to think about it is that the esoteric must be grounded in the baser forms of reality. *We are such stuff as dreams are made on.* The esoteric is built on top of the exoteric. Without it, the dreams float away into thin air. That is Shakespeare's warning to the first group of his audience, the one which can truly understand the esoteric in all its richness.

The second group are the direct opposite of the first in the sense that they are incapable of telling the difference between illusion and reality. The three revolutionaries represent the base instincts of human nature. Caliban is the unchecked sex drive, as seen in his attempt to rape Miranda. Stephano is a drunk, Trinculo a joker. When these instincts are kept under the guidance of wisdom and authority, as represented by Prospero and Antonio, they are no problem and can be made to do useful work. But it is when authority and wisdom disappear that the base instincts get out of hand and threaten to destroy everything. The martial authority of the Ruler is needed to prevent this outcome. But what we see in The Tempest is that the illusions of the Sage are equally effective. Thus, Prospero uses his illusions to control the base characters.

There is one of the three revolutionaries who needs a more specific interpretation, and that is Caliban. His story is that he was the son of a witch who was on the island when Prospero and Miranda arrived. Prospero turned Caliban into a faithful servant and this state of affairs continued until Miranda came of age at which point Caliban took a sexual interest in her which turned the relationship sour. As a result, Prospero now governs Caliban in a tyrannical fashion which has fuelled bitterness and resentment in the latter.

As with everything in The Tempest, there is a multi-faceted symbolism at play here. The dynamic between Caliban, Miranda, and Prospero makes sense in terms of the standard familial practices of the time that have appeared multiple times in our analysis. Caliban is an inappropriate love interest who is unacceptable to the father. Prospero is doing his job by protecting his daughter from such a man while also performing the same role as Leonato, Lord Capulet, and King Lear in finding a suitable husband for his daughter in the person of Ferdinand.

However, we know that Miranda is a symbol for the portion of Shakespeare's audience that is now mature enough to understand the esoteric. Prospero is leading Miranda and Ferdinand towards an understanding of that while deliberately preventing Caliban from attaining the same thing. Why? Because Caliban cannot be trusted with the knowledge. He will use it for evil instead of good. Caliban's lineage as the descendent of a witch is important because he is capable of understanding the esoteric. And that is actually what Caliban wants. He wants the power of the esoteric. His desire to kill Prospero and take over the island is his desire to master the art of magic and use it for his own purposes. Here, again, we see obvious parallels with Shakespearean characters who use illusion and deception for evil ends: the three witches in Macbeth, Iago, Claudius, and Don John.

Prospero's desire to suppress Caliban is symbolic of the real danger that can occur when the illusions of the Sage are used for evil instead of good. But what is even more poignant is that Caliban himself can't really tell the difference between illusion and reality. That was also true of Macbeth and the other characters just mentioned. But we can be even more specific. For such characters, illusion and magic are the projection of their own will. Their power comes from the fact that they can project their will to whatever end they desire. Will and illusion then become inseparable. Prospero must withhold the power of the esoteric from those who would be consumed by it.

If Miranda and Ferdinand represent the audience who are capable of understanding the meaning of art, magic, and illusion, and the three rogues are those who cannot and must not be allowed to understand it, what about the third group: the nobles who have done wrong? This is the group who allows the lust for power to overcome all else but who still has a conscience capable of understanding. For this group, the purpose of art and illusion is a moral, redemptive one. The artist simply holds up a mirror to their sins and allows conscience to do the rest. We have also seen this dynamic before. It is what Hamlet does to Claudius when he organises the play that shows exactly the same crime that the king committed against his brother. But there is a key difference to how this plays out in The Tempest.

Hamlet's trick doesn't work on Claudius. Even though it does act as a trigger for his conscience, he is unable to work his own way to redemption, and that is because he is still in power and the requirements of holding onto power trump the more esoteric concerns. This is exactly how Shakespeare structures the famous scene in the chapel. Claudius genuinely wants to seek redemption, but the practical matters of governance interrupt him. The same is true of Macbeth, who overrules his conscience in order to hold onto power at any price. It is no coincidence, therefore, that what occurs in The Tempest is that Prospero organises a shipwreck for Alonso, Antonio and the others. He sees to it that they are removed from the everyday business of life. Only then are they in the receptive frame of mind to be shown the truth and to have the time and space to digest it. Only then can they fully work through the difficult process of finding redemption.

To the extent that all of us are sinners who have done wrong in life, this redemptive power of art applies to us all. Art takes us away from everyday concerns and holds up a mirror in which we may see ourselves in both positive and negative aspects. In this respect, the fact that the other characters in the story seem to lack agency and are beholden to Prospero is not necessarily a power imbalance but one that is chosen. In the real world, nobody is forced to partake in art, but, if we do, we give our agency over to the "illusions" of the artist. This has been the role of the Sage in every culture throughout history. The archetype functions as the carrier of the highest truths and is ideally in an ongoing dialogue with the other members of society.

That is the societal viewpoint on the matter. But the symbolism works equally well for the individual. We may think of the Sage as a component of our psyche that maps to our conscience, our ability to love, and our recognition of truth and beauty. But it is more than that because the Sage is the unifying and holistic force that creates the holy state by mastering the other components of being. This is what is signified by the fact that Prospero controls everything in the story and leads everything towards a happy ending. His task is to harmonise the drives and desires manifested in the other characters. To the extent that he succeeds, he creates himself as a work of art. His relationships with his daughter and son-in-law, his servants, his butler, his jester, and even his enemies are all brought into a holy state at the end.

What Shakespeare shows us in The Tempest is that art has an integrating function that can bring all the elements of human nature together. It is art that makes holy, but the power of art, and what distinguishes it from philosophy and certain kinds of religion, is that it does not deny the sacred. On the contrary, the art of Shakespeare foregrounds the sacred part of the journey.

It is this foregrounding of the sacred that is behind Shakespeare's extensive use of covert exposition which, as a technique, allows him to place the starting state of the hero before the action of the story and thereby focus all the attention on the sacred part of the transformation cycle. Shakespeare's work, more than any before him, concentrates on the sacred and esoteric aspects of human existence. That is perfectly fitting for a Sage. But Shakespeare does not want the Sage to deny the exoteric aspects of existence. This brings us to the final meta-meaning implied by The Tempest. Prospero deliberately and wilfully brings the story to an end by giving up the esoteric power of the Sage and choosing to return back to the exoteric world of the Ruler. Since we know that Prospero had started out as a Ruler twelve years earlier, what we are shown in The Tempest is nothing more or less than the transformation cycle itself.

Prospero began his journey as the Ruler of Milan. That is his starting holy state. His transition into the sacred was triggered by the betrayal of his brother which destroyed his exoteric identity. His time on the island signifies the entirety of his journey into the sacred. He was away from home in a place he did not understand. He met strange creatures and learned to get along with them. He learned to rule over half-beasts like Caliban and spirits like Ariel. He learned to come to terms with the irrational and unconscious aspects of life. He became master of them. Now that he has mastered them, he is ready to return back to the exoteric world of the Ruler, which is another way to say, back to holy state.

All of the characters in The Tempest may therefore be seen to represent the dangers of the sacred state and the way we may become lost and unable to find our way back to the holy. Like Ariel and Ferdinand, we may want to disappear entirely into dissimulation and illusion. Like Stephano, we may just want to get rolling drunk and forget our cares. Like Trinculo, we may turn everything into a joke. Like Caliban, we may become bitter and resentful. Like Sebastian, we may begin plotting more trouble. Each of these can be thought of exoterically as people who exist in society or as symbols of esoteric tendencies we must overcome as individuals. Prospero has overcome them both individually and socially. He harmonises them all and guides them back into holy state. That is the role of the Sage. The Sage is the master of the sacred but must relinquish that power when the transformation cycle ends and the return to holy state is required.

There is one final feature of The Tempest to note: Prospero makes the journey alone in that he is entirely responsible for what happens. In Shakespeare's other comedies, it is not the hero who saves the day but one of the other characters (e.g., Friar Francis in Much Ado About Nothing). The characters in Shakespeare who are made to go it alone invariably come to ruin, even the greatest such as Hamlet and King Lear. But Prospero alone is responsible for guiding his story to a happy conclusion. Therefore, we may say that Prospero is Shakespeare's portrait of the self-actualised individual who has learned to navigate his way through life's journey by achieving what Shakespeare's tragic characters are unable to: reunite the esoteric and exoteric aspects of his identity. Prospero is the artist who is able to harmonise both his own inner nature and that of society towards the production of truth and beauty.

Because Prospero transitions from Ruler to Sage and back, we can see that Shakespeare does not see these as independent archetypes but as two sides of the same coin. What we should name the coin? Let's call it: the Artist. The Artist is both Sage and Ruler, esoteric and exoteric combined, controller of illusions and master of the material world. It is the Artist who sits above the lower transformation cycles, guiding, orchestrating, and harmonising them. But the Artist is also the hero in his own cycle and must also take the journey into the sacred. When Prospero chooses to return to society, he regains holy state, but this is just a precursor to the next transformation.

The fact that Shakespeare finished his career with a work such as The Tempest implies an overall optimism about the capacities of man. Nobody can accuse Shakespeare of avoiding the most difficult questions of life, but he ended on a positive note.

And this leads to a final remarkable fact as it relates to the notion of the Artist and the correspondence between Prospero and Shakespeare. The Tempest ends with Prospero turning to the audience and asking to be released from the bonds of entertaining them. Obviously, this was Shakespeare signing off from his career as a playwright. But if Shakespeare is Prospero, and if Prospero ends the story by deliberately giving up his role as Sage in order to go back to being a Ruler, there is another symbolic correspondence here between life and art.

Shakespeare was in his late forties when he wrote The Tempest. He had become a wealthy man and no doubt had a great deal of business to attend to in the "real world". In other words, he was making his own transition back to the "Ruler" by giving up writing in order to manage his own affairs. The most gifted writer in the English language retired early, just as King Lear did. Did Shakespeare have a plan similar to Lear's? Well, at the very least, he had one unmarried daughter who needed a husband.

Whatever plans Shakespeare had for the next phase of his life, they were cut short when he died unexpectedly just a few years later at fifty-two years of age. As Shakespeare well knew, because he taught us in King Lear, life often has other ideas for us than the ones we make for ourselves. We might well say that Shakespeare ended up like Lear.

But that is not exactly true. As an Artist-Sage, Shakespeare ended his journey on his own terms. Just like Prospero, he successfully guided his illusions back to holy state. That is the triumph that The Tempest represents. And four centuries later, we are still – like Miranda and Ferdinand – bedazzled, mystified, and uplifted by them.

Conclusion: King Lear vs Oedipus

We began this book by presenting a model that, by building on the extensive comparative scholarship of Joseph Campbell, purports to be a universal of human culture. The notion of story-as-transformation, when generalised to include any and all aspects of human identity, can capture the full range of transformations that we go through in life, from the most minor everyday surprises through to the full-blown identity crises that Shakespeare shows us. One of the themes we have pursued throughout the book is the differences between Shakespeare and the Renaissance literature that was a major inspiration for him. That raises the notion that, even though the structure of transformations may be universal, it is also true that the great stories of any culture represent that culture's understanding of the world manifested in the way it represents and understands its own specific set of transformations. It will be a fitting way for us to summarise the main themes that we have found in Shakespeare by drawing out this notion of cultural differences in a comparison of his tragic works against those which emerged in ancient Greek culture.

Commentators such as Harold Bloom have credited Shakespeare with creating that modern mentality. Whether that is true or whether he was a mirror for what was already emerging is not a question that can be answered. What is certainly true is that an understanding of the qualities that are unique in Shakespeare can tell us a great deal about the culture which began in his time but which has arguably come to fruition in ours. In comparing the Shakespearean tragedy against that of the ancient Greeks, there are any number of works we could choose from, however, since we have spent a great deal of time in this book working through the true meaning of King Lear, since Sophocles' Oedipus Rex is almost certainly the greatest of the Greek tragedies, and since both stories feature kings who lose their kingdoms and are betrayed by their progeny, there can be no better point of comparison. Let's begin by applying our analytical model to the great work of Sophocles.

The briefest summary of Oedipus Rex will suffice for our purposes. When the story begins, Oedipus is the king of Thebes. A plague is devastating his land, so the king sends his brother-in-law to ask the oracle for advice. The oracle says that the cause of the plague is the fact that the murderer of the former king, Laius, has not been found. Oedipus sets out to find the murderer, not knowing that it is he himself who killed Laius in a former incident. Oedipus also doesn't know that Laius was his real father or that his current wife, Jocasta, was the former wife of the king and is therefore his mother. His investigations eventually reveal the truth to him. He gouges out his eyes in despair and begs to be exiled. The play ends with the chorus telling the audience that no man is happy until he is dead.

If we apply our now familiar methodology to the story, we can see that Oedipus begins in sacred state to the extent that he has committed some of the worst offences possible: patricide and incest. Nevertheless, because he and the other characters are completely unaware of this, it is more accurate to say that he begins the story in holy state, doing exactly what he should be doing as a king, which is trying to eradicate the plague from his kingdom and alleviate the suffering of his people. This establishes one of the dominant themes in the story, which is that Oedipus is an exemplary man. From his point of view, and from the point of view of any normal Greek of his time, he always acts according to what is virtuous and right. Nevertheless, he is brought undone.

The first sign of an identity crisis, and also the first indication that Oedipus is not entirely a saint, comes when he gets into an argument with a seer and falsely concludes that his brother-in-law, Creon, has paid the man to work against him. This leads Oedipus to demand that Creon be put to death. Fortunately, he is persuaded otherwise. However, at the same time, Oedipus gets the first hint that he might have been the one who killed Laius. The investigation which started as a way to solve the problem of the plague has taken a personal twist. The rest of the story sees Oedipus pursuing the matter even as some of the lesser characters who know the truth try to keep it from him.

Here we see a fascinating variation on the journey into the sacred part of the story. As we have already mentioned, Oedipus' identity is already in sacred state at the start in the sense that his and everybody else's understanding is wrong. He is quite simply not who he thinks he is. Note that it is his familial identity where the true problem lies. Oedipus' understanding of his lineage is incorrect, as is his knowledge about his own wife. Now, none of this matters from an exoteric point of view. His identity is stable, and he has carried out his duties exactly as he should. What is going to cause the problem is his search for the truth, which is an esoteric journey.

Thus, we have the classic imbalance between the exoteric and esoteric that marks the journey into the sacred. However, while the investigation is ongoing and while the journey into the sacred is taking place, Oedipus himself is mostly unaware of the trouble he has gotten himself into. It is the audience who knows what is going on. Therefore, we might actually say that the journey into the sacred is primarily targeted to the audience. This is exactly how Aristotle describes the play in the Poetics. He talks about tragedy primarily as an art form that evokes pity from the audience. The audience knows Oedipus is doomed. Oedipus does not. As we will see shortly, this is the first major difference between Greek and Shakespearean tragedy.

Oedipus' journey into the sacred finally comes to an end when he learns the truth about his past. At that point, his exoteric identity is completely destroyed. Clearly, he can no longer be king. His mother/wife Jocasta commits suicide. His daughters are exiled. Later, his sons will go to war against each other. In despair, Oedipus blinds himself, but this is symbolic of the fact that the one thing he has attained from the whole journey is the truth, a truth which has destroyed him. The story invites us to believe that he could have remained happy and whole if not for his desire to seek the truth. Thus, we can say that Oedipus sacrifices his identity for truth.

We might be tempted to say that this puts Oedipus on a par with Shakespearean heroes such as Hamlet who are also seeking truth. But there are some of the major differences that exist between the worldview of the Greeks and that of Shakespeare. Hamlet is seeking the truth in order to pursue justice against his uncle Claudius. Oedipus is pursuing a truth that is going to bring himself to justice. Some of the other characters in the story know that, which is why they are trying to keep the truth from Oedipus. They are not acting out of self-interest but out of what they believe is best for the king. By contrast, the other characters in Hamlet are not trying to keep the truth from the prince. With the exception of Claudius, they simply don't know what the truth is. For the Greeks, truth was always exoteric and universal in nature. It was what everybody could agree on. In Shakespeare, the truth is private and therefore not able to be shared. Oedipus is ruined because a truth that was private becomes public. Hamlet desires to bring a private truth into the light of day but fails to do so because there is nobody to help him with his task.

The esoteric nature of truth pervades all of Shakespeare's work. It is not just a function of the way that the characters interact with each other but also how we as the audience interact with the story. Consider the technique of covert exposition. We have seen that this makes it far more difficult for the audience to understand the story because it requires attention to detail and the ability to reason through what is only implied and never explained directly. Indeed, in the case of Hamlet and Lear, it is the failure to understand the covert exposition that has meant those stories have remained misinterpreted for four centuries. The meaning has always been there, but it has remained private.

Nothing could be further from the mentality of the Greeks than these private meanings and truths. Indeed, there is no exposition at all in Oedipus Rex because the story itself had been around since time immemorial and everybody in the audience already knew its basic outline. While it is true that Sophocles made several important modifications, most importantly by highlighting Oedipus' search for truth and his responsibility for his own undoing, none of that is hidden from the audience. On the contrary, one of the main effects of Oedipus Rex is that the audience already knows the outcome before it has happened. The truth is already public. It is for the hero to learn the truth that everybody else already knows.

Compare this against King Lear. The nature of the story of Lear has been contested ever since it was premiered. Some of the greatest minds of the last several hundred years have not agreed on the meaning of the work. To this day, the truth is still not agreed upon. That is true of the larger discussion that has taken place in the general culture, but it is also true of the characters in the story. They do not understand what Lear is trying to do either. The truth in Lear is hidden and can only be deciphered by the kind of sophisticated analysis we have provided in this book. Even then, there will be those who disagree. But nobody disagrees about the meaning of Oedipus Rex. Only in the most abstract sense can there be any debate about it.

Lear's truth is not exoteric. It is intensely personal. He believes that the kingdom will not survive the succession of any of his daughters if he allows them to rule alone. Even if Lear were to share this truth with others, they would almost certainly disagree with him. Thus, the truth that sets events in motion is private in nature. Meanwhile, the truth that gets the story moving for Oedipus is one that all can see. There is a plague. No sophisticated model of reality is required to see that. Any village idiot can figure it out. We have a contrast between exoteric, simple truths and esoteric, complex ones.

Related to this is the temporal aspect. Oedipus' immediate problem is in the present with the plague that is ravaging his kingdom. He sets out to solve that but ends up pursuing a truth that is in the past, namely, the formative events of his own identity. Those events have already happened, he just needs to learn to see them for what they really are.

Lear's truth is neither in the past nor present. It is in the future. It is a truth about what will happen once he dies and passes the kingdom on to the next generation. For that reason, it is inherently speculative. There is no guarantee that what Lear believes will come to pass. Other calamities or events may intervene to prevent the outcome that he foresees. The speculative nature of the truth means that Lear cannot be absolutely certain about it. That's another reason why he cannot share his truth with others, because they could quite legitimately argue that it will not happen that way and there is no evidence that could decide the matter one way or another. Meanwhile, Oedipus spends the entirety of the story meticulously collecting the evidence that will prove the truth he is searching for.

Thus, we see a clear distinction here between two worldviews. In Oedipus, truth is exoteric, public, universal, and empirical. In Lear, it is esoteric, private, individual, and speculative. Lear goes to his death without having shared his truth with anybody else in the story, and it has remained unknown for the last four hundred years in Western culture. By contrast, Oedipus learns a truth which the audience already knows. The truth becomes universal at the end of the story. In a sense, Oedipus has strayed from the truth and needs to be brought back into the fold. Lear simply has a different truth altogether, and, even though his truth is proven entirely correct by the events that follow his removal from power, it doesn't save the day, because it is only a partial truth. Lear did not foresee everything, and what he does not know brings him undone.

We might conclude that there is a scepticism towards truth in Shakespeare. The truth does not save Lear, and it does not save Hamlet. Their possession of it is no guarantee of success. That is why it is partial and speculative. When Oedipus is brought undone by the truth, that in no way invalidates it. On the contrary, the story reaffirms the idea of truth in the fact that Oedipus recognises it although he has every reason not to do so. This notion is reinforced in the next play in the Theban trilogy, Oedipus at Colonus, where the now blind and exiled ex-king becomes a source of wisdom. Oedipus has suffered for the truth. He now carries it with him and will impart it to the next generation. The victory of Theseus and the fall of Creon are based on the fact that one venerates the truth and the other shuns it. All of this reaffirms the sanctity of truth.

These differences in worldview exist even though both kings have the same goal: the preservation of their kingdom. Oedipus is trying to stop the plague. Lear is trying to prevent a civil war. War, plague, and famine have beleaguered rulers for all of history. For the vast majority of history, all anybody could do was to batten down the hatches and wait for the storm to pass. Oedipus is at least proactive in seeking a resolution to the plight of his people. That reinforces his adherence to truth and his virtuous nature. In Lear, we see something very different. Lear creates the storm that will engulf his kingdom. He is a king who rules over a nation that is at peace. That is why he has the time and intellect to think ahead and see future problems before they occur. He then plans a course of action that he hopes will prevent calamity. But the only way to prevent a large calamity is to create a smaller one.

The evidence from Greek and Roman history suggests that they responded to crises in the same way that Oedipus does, i.e., they waited for a problem to arise and then threw everything at it. Lear is not waiting for the problem to come. He is trying to reorganise things so it never eventuates in the first place. A side effect of this is that Lear becomes entirely responsible for what happens. By becoming himself the cause of events, Lear is accountable for all the consequences that occur, even the ones he could never have foreseen.

It may not be immediately obvious, but these differences are a side effect of each culture's orientation to truth. The universal truth of the Greeks was completely impersonal. No individual could be responsible for the truth, only for their violation of it. Oedipus must learn that the hard way, and he is brought back into submission to the truth by the end of the story. That is what is represented by the fact that he is completely innocent of his actions. Oedipus is not personally responsible for anything that occurs to him because not only did he have no knowledge of what he was doing, he acted in a way that any other Greek of his time would have done. The myth of the blind king, which every Greek knew, proves this.

Oedipus was out walking when he was almost run down by a man in a chariot, who then proceeded to whip him without provocation. Oedipus' murder of Laius was done in ignorance of the identity of his attacker and self-defence at the man's actions. Therefore, he cannot be morally culpable. The same goes for his relationship with his mother. The marriage occurred after Oedipus solved the riddle of the Sphinx. It was bestowed on him by the people of Thebes who needed a new king. Marriage to the former king's wife was part of the deal. Thus, not only was Oedipus not morally culpable, he was acting in a manner that was fully in accordance with virtue. The story makes crystal clear that it cannot be a matter of responsibility. Oedipus is being held to account, but not because of his wilful actions.

We might argue that Lear is also acting in a way that is worthy of praise since he is trying to prevent a civil war. But, even if we agree with this intent, his actions are morally questionable, and a strong case could be made that they are reprehensible since he ends up trying to foment a civil war where one did not yet exist. Not only is Lear's truth speculative from the point of view of cause and effect and whether it can lead to the outcome he desires, it is at least ethically ambiguous. That is yet another reason why Lear cannot share his plan with others. They would object on moral grounds. Therefore, Lear's responsibility is both causal and moral. However, since nobody else knows what he is doing, he faces no public censure. It is never a question of Lear being judged according to social or universal truths. His journey into the sacred already places himself outside any such criteria. Just like Macbeth, Lear is answerable only to his conscience.

All of this gives us a number of criteria which summarise the major differences between Greek and Shakespearean tragedy. There are questions of truth, intentionality, foresight, and responsibility. The Greeks have an orientation towards the past and present. Shakespeare is orientated towards the future. On the question of consciousness, Oedipus is not conscious of what he is getting himself into. He only becomes conscious at the end of the story. When he does so, he is brought back into the public consciousness represented by the audience and the chorus. There is a kind of communal catharsis at play in Greek tragedy. That's why it is the chorus which has the last word in Oedipus Rex.

We have already noted that what differentiates Shakespeare's heroes is their clarity of consciousness they have in advance of the transformation they are undertaking. They are conscious of the sacrifice and identity crisis at the start, and they remain conscious throughout the journey into the sacred. All this heightens their intentionality and therefore their responsibility. Everything Lear does in the first two acts of the story is done on purpose. This is true even of his baiting of Goneril and their subsequent argument where Lear says a number of incredibly hurtful things to his own daughter. Lear's willingness to hurt his daughter is mirrored in his willingness to risk throwing his kingdom into civil war. The degree of responsibility that comes with this is immense, but all the more so because he alone knows the plan. Consciousness in Shakespeare rests with the hero. In Greek tragedy, it rests with the public.

All of these differences exist even though the stories of the two kings have so much in common. Lear and Oedipus both come undone. They both lose their identity as king and father. They both struggle to ensure the security of their children but are also betrayed by some of them. Their fall from power causes war that leads to death and destruction on a societal scale. All of these properties are shared between their stories. And, yet, we have just summarised vast differences between the two cultures as embodied in the character of the king. In Oedipus, we have the exemplary man who has done exactly what he should have done at every stage of the journey. His downfall is no fault of his own. The primary theme here is fate and the fact that the vicissitudes of life are such that virtue is no guarantee of success. Nevertheless, the story upholds the idea of truth and virtue as abstract concepts that are still valid and correct. This is shown by Oedipus' determined search to understand the truth even though it will ruin him. To face truth with courage and resolve was perhaps the highest ideal communicated in Sophocles' stories of Oedipus. Despite his ruin, Oedipus is an example to be followed.

We argued earlier that Lear becomes an example for Edgar to follow, but this is not true in the sense of him being either a worldly authority or a source of wisdom and eternal truth. On the contrary, Lear and Edgar meet on the heath as madmen. No information is exchanged between them, no knowledge or wisdom. Edgar neither learns from Lear the truth about what has happened nor any general truths. What Edgar gets to see is something deeper and more fundamental. He sees a man who has lost his exoteric identity entirely but in whom some fire still burns. Lear and Edgar experience the parts of human nature that exist where no intelligence, wisdom, and authority can penetrate. If wisdom and reason are like the light of the sun, these other properties can only be discovered at night on the heath in a storm. It is this which we have called the sacred, and it is this which separates Shakespeare from the classical tradition. The Greek tragedy takes place in the noonday sun of reason. Shakespeare's takes place under a full moon where the light of reason and logic is but a reflection, a light in the rear-view mirror.

Thus, while it is a universal that every story entails a journey into the sacred that requires the hero to transform themselves, we can now see that Shakespeare emphasises the sacred part of the transformation, its esoteric, inner dimensions. That is why it is no coincidence that the Bard made such extensive use of covert exposition in his works. His two greatest heroes in Hamlet and Lear are already in sacred state when we meet them, not just in the sense that their transformation has already begun but in their own understanding. They have already taken a step into a world where reason and logic can no longer help them. If we view them from the safety and security of reason, we cannot understand them. They are already sacred, un-whole, and unholy. Their stories are ever-evolving, ever-changing, dynamic, and in flux. The "truths" that exist at the end are not those that were there at the beginning.

For the Greeks, the playing out of fate was tragic because of its mechanical certainty and inevitability. Every piece of knowledge gets Oedipus one step closer to the revelation that will ruin him. The audience knows it's coming. That's the whole point. There is no dynamism at play, no new piece of information that changes anything. For that reason, there is also no hope, which is why courage and fortitude are foregrounded.

Shakespeare provides hope, not out of any absence of courage, but as a result of the fact that the outcome of his journey into the sacred cannot be known. At the end of the story, Hamlet is one step away from proving Claudius a murderer. Lear reunites with Cordelia, and for a moment it seems like everything might be okay. Even in the death of the hero, Shakespeare's journey into the sacred is an optimistic one compared to the Greeks precisely because knowledge and truth are in no way fixed. But, to say it again, this optimism is not trivial or delusional. Neither is it easy. In fact, it is a source of potential horror. The sacred is terrifying because it transcends the categories of reason. It can produce monstrosities like Iago and Macbeth, but it can also delight and enrapture like the illusions of Prospero.

Oedipus was the Greeks' highest ideal: the man who searches for a truth that is knowable by all and then upholds it even when it ruins him. Lear starts with a truth which is private and known only to himself. He then willingly destroys his own identity in an attempt to create a new world where that truth no longer holds. Shakespeare's heroes consciously take the journey into the sacred in an attempt to transcend "truth" and "fate". That is true even of Don Pedro in Much Ado About Nothing, who is trying to create a world that is full of love rather than leave it up to the whims of the gods. Romeo and Juliet are trying to transcend the enmity of their families. Hamlet is trying to inject esoteric truth and justice into a mechanical kingdom that operates entirely on appearances. Macbeth no longer wishes to be the faithful servant and longs to be master. Iago will destroy the system by weaponising his talents against those who are blind to them. Each, in their own way, is deliberately trying to transcend the status quo.

Oedipus is a man who has unwittingly strayed from the path of virtue and whose reconciliation with truth brings him back into line with his society. Shakespeare's heroes willingly place themselves outside the pale. They do so because they are not just trying to transform themselves but also their society too. The success of their journey is made far less likely by the fact that it requires both microcosmic and macrocosmic transformations. Therefore, the failure of the hero is always mirrored in the failure of the broader social transformation. Romeo and Juliet's death extinguishes esoteric love in Verona. Hamlet's death destroys the chance of truth and justice in Denmark. Macbeth's death may seem to end the bloodshed in Scotland, but we know that Banquo's son is destined to recommence it later.

All of this would be nihilistic were it not for the character of the witness as the embodiment of Shakespearean truth. To say it one last time, Greek truth was contained in the chorus. It was public and universal. Shakespearean truth is manifested in the hero but, perhaps more importantly, in the witness who is the only one that understands the journey into the sacred that has been taken. The witness must grasp not eternal truths but private ones. They must know the identity crisis that the hero has faced, the willing sacrifice they undertook, and the goal for which they strived. But these starting points do not remain static. The journey into the sacred changes the parameters of truth itself. Therefore, truth can only lie in the journey as a whole. The unit of truth is the entire process that has occurred. It is the transformation. It is the story.

This is fundamentally different from the Greek conception of truth as fixed and static. Only if we measure Shakespeare against such purported eternal truths is he nihilistic. If we can get over that, what we find is actually a far more optimistic view of a world where transformation is possible and where new things may arise. In this world, truth and justice may emerge. The esoteric love of Romeo and Juliet and Othello and Desdemona may be celebrated. The great illusions of Prospero may tantalise, delight, and instruct. None of these existed prior. They must be created from scratch. Therefore, there is always the risk of failure. But the nominal failure of a Shakespearean hero is counterbalanced by the fact that they have learned something in the attempt to transform themselves and their world. The task of the witness is to ensure that what has been learned does not die with the hero. That is the meaning of the exchange between Horatio and Hamlet after the prince is fatally wounded:

O good Horatio, what a wounded name,
(Things standing thus unknown) shall live behind me.
If thou didst ever hold me in thy heart,
Absent thee from felicity a while,
And in this harsh world draw thy breath in pain,
To tell my story.

Horatio must tell the story because Shakespearean truth lies in the story. It is the full transformation of the hero from start to finish, including and especially the intention which began the journey. That is why we fail to understand Shakespeare's heroes when we don't understand their intention. Instead, we say they are going mad. Lear is mad. Hamlet is a half-mad depressive. Our own failure to grasp intention leads us to these conclusions. It follows that Shakespearean truth is incredibly fragile. The hero takes the journey alone, and there remains a single solitary witness at the end to carry the torch forward. What must be grasped is the intent. What is crucial is that Lear tries to save his kingdom and that Hamlet tries to obtain truth and justice.

The transmission of truth by the witness is not just an academic retelling of facts, it is an invitation to pick up the mantle left by the fallen hero and carry it forward. That is precisely what Edgar does at the end of Lear. He does not do so out of duty or authority to the fallen king but because he has been a witness to his story and has felt the same fire that burns even when all exoteric appearances have been lost.

Over and above the specific details of these stories, there rest these higher truths of Shakespearean art which differentiate it from what came before and which have come to signify the core truths of modern Western culture: intentionality, consciousness, individuality, responsibility, and a willingness to transform ourselves. This gives our culture its dynamism but comes at the price of relinquishing the eternal truths of the past for a truth which evolves and changes, in which one never feels secure and safe, and which requires a constant re-evaluation. All of this can make one nauseous. This new truth has its enormous dangers in nihilism, confusion, lies and deceits, propaganda, loneliness, and so many of the other factors that are present in our time. These are all properties of the journey into the sacred as Shakespeare understood it. He did not shy away from them, but he also showed what it means to transcend them and find our way back to holy state with a truth that is no longer eternal but which evolves and opens outwards into new possibilities. To master the cycle of transformation is to learn how to create oneself and one's world. The process is fraught with danger, but that is the price of admission to the journey into the sacred.

About the Author

For information about upcoming releases and a regular blog, visit my website at https://simonsheridan.me

You can connect with me on:

- https://simonsheridan.me

Also by Simon Sheridan

The Initiation of Nietzsche: Wagner's Disciple

Is it possible to live your life as if it were a work of art? Can we go one step further and become the authors of our own lives rather than side characters in another's story? These were the dangerous ideas that Richard Wagner used to "corrupt" a bright young philology student named Friedrich Nietzsche. Just as Socrates corrupted Plato into becoming the founder of Western philosophy, so would Wagner corrupt Nietzsche into becoming one of the philosophical giants of the modern age. In the terms that we will use in this book, Wagner initiated Nietzsche. This book tells the story of their relationship in the only that really makes sense: as a work of art.

Archetypology: The Archetypal Study of Human Nature

In this introductory volume, Simon Sheridan outlines a framework for understanding human nature that places the concept of the archetype at the centre of analysis. The model revolves around four primary archetypes inspired by the psychology of Carl Jung - the Child, the Orphan, the Adult, and the Elder. With these and just a few other core concepts, archetypology provides a succinct but powerful framework that expands the archetype concept beyond the psychological to integrate nominally discrete domains such as biology, anthropology, history, and literature. The result is a holistic account of human development centred around the pattern of the cycle-ending-in-transcendence.

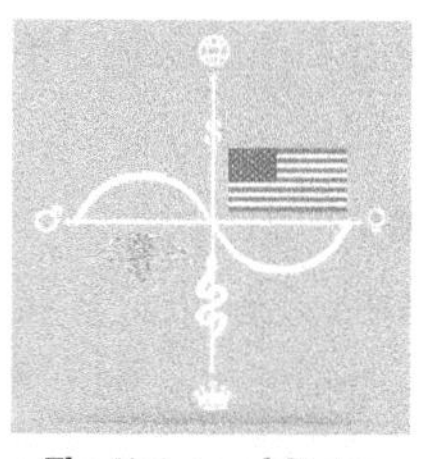

The Universal State of America: An Archetypal Calculus of Western Civilisation

In this sequel to his 2021 book, The Devouring Mother: The Collective Unconscious in the Time of Corona, author Simon Sheridan follows the archetypal breadcrumbs in search of the historical basis for the psychological drivers that increasingly dominate our modern world. Drawing on the work of the great comparative scholars Joseph Campbell, Arnold van Gennep, Oswald Spengler, and Arnold Toynbee, Sheridan expands the concept of the archetype beyond the domain of psychology to integrate biology, anthropology, literature, and, especially, history. The result is a unique synthesis that posits that the unfolding of civilisation proceeds according to the same pattern as an individual human life: a cyclical process punctuated by dramatic periods of transcendence.

The Devouring Mother: The Collective Unconscious in the Time of Corona

Those who fail to incorporate the shadow are doomed to project it. In the modern materialist West, we don't merely fail to incorporate our shadow, we deny its existence. In The Devouring Mother, author Simon Sheridan takes a journey into the other half of the psyche looking for an archetypal explanation for the social ructions in western society over the last several years beginning with the Trump and Brexit votes and reaching earthquake proportions with the corona event.

The Plague Story and Other Essays: Re-Evaluating the Coronavirus Narrative

Societies run on stories. But in the modern west, we believe that we are above stories; we are scientific. It is partly because of this (story!) that we are often blind to the stories we tell ourselves. In this book, I analyse the structure of the story we have been telling ourselves about the corona event: the plague story. I look at how the plague story unfolded and who has been telling it. The structure of that story dictates both what has happened so far and what needs to happen to bring the matter to an end.

www.ingramcontent.com/pod-product-compliance
Lightning Source LLC
Chambersburg PA
CBHW051111050726
47592CB00002B/777

* 9 7 8 1 7 6 4 2 3 0 5 2 0 *